NUMEROLOGY FOR THE BEGINNER

Master the Secret Meaning of Numbers and Discover Your Future Through Numerology, Astrology and Tarot Reading

By
Michelle Northrup

© Copyright 2019 by Michelle Northrup - All rights reserved.

This content is provided with the sole purpose of providing relevant information on a specific topic for which every reasonable effort has been made to ensure that it is both accurate and reasonable. Nevertheless, by purchasing this content you consent to the fact that the author, as well as the publisher, are in no way experts on the topics contained herein, regardless of any claims as such that may be made within. As such, any suggestions or recommendations that are made within are done so purely for entertainment value. It is recommended that you always consult a professional prior to undertaking any of the advice or techniques discussed within.

This is a legally binding declaration that is considered both valid and fair by both the Committee of Publishers Association and the American Bar Association and should be considered as legally binding within the United States.

The reproduction, transmission, and duplication of any of the content found herein, including any specific or extended information will be done as an illegal act regardless of the end form the information ultimately takes. This includes copied versions of the work both physical, digital and audio unless express consent of the Publisher is provided beforehand. Any additional rights reserved.

Furthermore, the information that can be found within the pages described forthwith shall be considered both accurate and truthful when it comes to the recounting of facts. As such, any use, correct or incorrect, of the provided information will render the Publisher free of responsibility as to the actions taken outside of their direct purview. Regardless, there are zero scenarios where the original author or the Publisher can be deemed liable in any fashion for any damages or hardships that may result from any of the information discussed herein.

Additionally, the information in the following pages is intended only for informational purposes and should thus be thought of as universal. As befitting its nature, it is presented without assurance regarding its prolonged validity or interim quality. Trademarks that are mentioned are done without written consent and can in no way be considered an endorsement from the trademark holder.

Table of Contents

Introduction

Chapter 1 *A Self-Discovery Scientific Method*

Chapter 2 *Revealing Your Inner Self*

Chapter 3 *Individuality Arrows And Their Meaning*

Chapter 4 *Ruling And Day Numbers*

Chapter 5 *Your Peak And Pinnacle Years*

Chapter 6 *Connections Between Astrology And Numerology*

Chapter 7 *Connections Between Tarot And Numerology*

Chapter 8 *Relationship Compatibility*

Chapter 9 *Cycle Of Change*

Chapter 10 *Numbers For Money, Motivation, And Passion*

Conclusion

Description

INTRODUCTION

Thank you for choosing *Numerology for the Beginner: Master the Secret Meaning of Numbers and Discover Your Future through Numerology, Astrology, and Tarot Reading.* As you begin to explore Numerology more deeply in this introductory book, hopefully, you find insight and answers to who you are and your purpose in life. The numbers in your life do not "tell" the future, but they do shed insight into what themes underline your lives. You can use these vibrations or currents to learn about your true Self. This is how you can prepare for your future and support your present life.

As for all the various mystical sciences, Numerology is a generally simple practice. Once you understand how to calculate the various areas of interest and the general vibrations of the numbers one through nine, you will be able to find the thread of various traits that are woven throughout your life. While the process is simple, learning how to apply this knowledge and grow from it can be a challenge. Be warned, your numbers may reveal wonderful traits and secrets about yourself, but they may also reveal some hard challenges you face. There are good and bad traits we all possess. You can learn how to grow your strengths and improve your weaknesses if you learn how. Thankfully, in addition to revealing what your numbers mean, your readings and numbers can also help you learn how to grow.

Get ready to dig deeper into understanding yourself and your future by learning the basics of Numerology, and how it relates to other sciences like astrology and tarot. Come back for reference when you need it, especially when you experience a numerological change, to make sure you are moving confidently in the direction of your true Self and destiny.

There are plenty of books on this subject on the market, thanks again for choosing this one! Every effort was made to ensure it is full of as much useful information as possible, please enjoy!

CHAPTER 1
A Self-Discovery Scientific Method

You may have a vague idea of Numerology. For example, you may recognize the prefix, "number-," in the title and connect that it has something to do with numbers. Or maybe you see that it contains the suffix "-ology," identifying it as a scientific study of something. Together the name shares what it is, the study of numbers. But, the study of what numbers? And In what context? Where did it come from and how can you use it in your life? The answers to these questions are briefly discussed in this chapter for you and expanded further throughout this book.

For centuries it has been understood that numbers can be used to decode certain information and that each number has a certain vibrational quality. Knowing and understanding the life science of numerology, you hold the key to decoding things in your life so you can pursue and empower certain aspects of your environment. For example, you can support your relationships better, pursue a career well aligned with you, and even grow your spiritual life.

An added advantage of numerology is that it is simple to learn and apply. It studies the meaning of numbers from one to nine and sometimes includes the numbers 11 and 22. This means that if a number is outside of this range, it is assigned another number that is within this range. Therefore, you do not need to remember the meaning for a lot of different things, and you can apply it to just about anything in your life. Some people assign numbers to the alphabet, while others figure out the numbers of your birthday. There are many applications, some of which will be explored later in this book. It is an excellent science for learning more about you and your unique journey and great for those just starting a journey into metaphysics.

In addition to being a simple science to learn and apply, it is also a lot of fun! You can use your understanding of numeric symbolism and vibration to identify talents, strengths, opportunities, and even personality traits for yourself and others around you. You can understand how and why people behave the way they do, and also can learn how people will work and interact together. This is an incredibly beneficial skill, especially for those in a leadership role. Knowing a person's numbers and what those mean allows you to guide them effectively, supporting their strengths and developing their opportunities. You can communicate with them more effectively and align them better with their destined path.

The idea that numbers have vibrational qualities is neither far-fetched nor unrealistic. For example, we know and understand that colors have their own certain vibration. It is not unrealistic than to recognize that numbers have their own as well. It is like each number has its own musical note and score. Star Wars' musical score is an easily recognizable theme song. Each note combines in the score to make it intense and very serious. The same idea applies to numerology. Sometimes the numbers combine to make a strong vibration in your life, and sometimes they play a softer role. In addition, the position of a number in your life can be a circular influence or like a thread weaving through your entire life. It all depends on the number, the combination of your numbers, and how it is positioned.

This philosophy is an ancient science with roots still shrouded in mystery. Not all agree with how and where numerology began. There are some early records from Babylon and Egypt that was used to develop the Hebrew interpretation of numerology referred to as the "Chaldean" system. In addition to this, there is evidence of numerology being used thousands of years ago in Greece, Japan, Rome, and China. The most common development-story is often associated with Pythagoras, the Greek philosopher.

Both a mathematician and philosopher, Pythagoras was born in Greece about 590 BCE. He was respected for his intelligence and wisdom. Today you can still see his influence in the Pythagorean theorem in high school and college geometry classes. In addition to his influence with mathematics, Pythagoras is considered the "father" of modern numerology. Unfortunately, not much is recorded about the early years of Pythagoras. Some writings indicate that he was a charming man that most people liked interacting with. In addition, it is thought that he was also athletic, earning medals for agility in the Olympic games of the time.

Another fascinating detail later revealed about Pythagoras was his "secret society," or school, that he founded in Crotona, Italy. This group, called the "semi-circle," was for both men and women to study topics such as music, astronomy, and mathematics with him. It was said that the students were required to spend five years in total silence to stimulate their intense contemplation and firm faith. They were also not allowed to write down or record his teachings in any way. The only way we know about this private school is from records written down after his death.

Pythagoras' focus on mathematics was different than modern mathematical studies. Instead of trying to figure out the answer to a question, Pythagoras focused on the concepts behind the math. To him, numbers could be used to express everything in the universe. To help do this, Pythagoras developed a framework for this, which other Greek philosophers expanded upon later. His developments were not the creation of the science of numerology, but they did lead to significant advances in the field. It was his radical concepts that earned him the distinction of the "father of numerology."

Numerology remained a self- and universal-discovery scientific method for thousands of years, losing favor as more defined explanations took shape; however, in modern times Dr. Julia Stenton brought it back to the public, especially when she named it "numerology." The foundation of the science reveals how numbers can tell the story of the universe, but it is still a relatively unknown metaphysical science. Now it is mostly referenced for finding the secret meaning of everyday things as well as a means for predicting the future. What the history of numerology hints at; however, is that it is capable of far more than just this!

There are three "popular" types of numerology; Kabbalah, Chaldean, and Pythagorean. Of course, there are many more interpretations, but these three are the most common you will encounter in the public. While more will be shared on various types of numerology later, each is briefly explained for you here.

The Hebrew science of numerology is also called, "Kabbalah Numerology." Basically, the idea boils down to the understanding that the Ego, or a person's flesh or physical body, does not contain absolute knowledge. Instead, the mind and soul, or higher self, are the seat of wisdom. This type of numerology believes that there are 22 different vibrations and they range all the way to 400. It was developed from the Greek alphabet but now is adapted for the contemporary Roman alphabet. While it is distinct, it does have some reflection of the Pythagorean Numerology variation, explained further below.

Ancient Babylon had their own version of numerology, called the "Chaldean" method. Some of the names are interpreted the same as those in the Kabbalah method, and it also contains some astrological concepts as well. In this system, the number nine is a holy number. Unlike other systems, there are double digits allowed. A single digit represents a person's external characteristics while double digits identify the internal features.

The third most popular type of numerology is the Pythagorean Numerology. It is based on the ideas of Pythagoras directly. It is an intersection of Pythagoras' love for the spiritual world and mathematics. According to this method, like the Chaldean interpretation, a person's legal name and birthdate reveal an interesting interaction and revelation about who they truly are. The numbers used in this system are primarily one through nine, although there are two double-digit numbers used, 11 and 22.

More on Pythagorean Numerology

Because most modern numerology is based on the Pythagorean Numerology system, it is important that you have a strong foundational understanding of what it is and what it encompasses. More detail about the following concepts will be explained further on in this book; however, this is to serve as a beginning introduction to the concepts. It is also a way for you to begin to see the translation of the history of numerology and how it has evolved from thousands of years ago to what it is and how it is used today.

"All things are numbers," is a telling quote shared by Pythagoras more than 2,000 years ago. Some people claim he learned the idea of numerology while in India and studying with Indian gurus, while others claim it was while he was in Egypt. Regardless of how he learned it, he used his mathematical intellect to radically change the view of the metaphysical study of numerology for us all.

According to him, each number had a special meaning and numbers were also a spiritual expression on Earth. For Pythagoras and his students or followers, numbers were a way to find and converse with God.

Below is a very basic breakdown for each number, one through ten:
- 1 = The beginning of everything
- 2 = Matter and the physical self
- 3 = The "ideal" number
- 4 = Each of the four elements and the four seasons
- 5 = Marriage and union
- 7 = The "sacred" number
- 10 = The "perfect" number

He was so ingrained in this belief system that he never appeared to gather in groups larger than ten people. He was a very spiritual person and made sure that the interpretation of the numbers surrounding him aligned with his spiritual beliefs and what he believed to be best for his students.

Today, the Roman alphabet is assigned specific numbers with distinct meanings. A person's legal name can then be analyzed to identify personal motivations, natural expressions, and how you make impressions on other people who come in contact with you. This means that when you are named at birth you are "assigned" specific tools and abilities, as well as ingrained talents, linked to your name. There is nothing clairvoyant or psychic about this process; it is an intuitive application of numbers to letters that reveal a person's ability. For those that follow the Pythagorean numerology science, a full name at birth is necessary to identify and "assign" these traits immediately.

When determining your Pythagorean numerology, you will have six primary numbers. There are three associated with your name, and three associated with your birth date. The six numbers are then used to reveal exactly who you are and how you can live your best life. In addition to the six numbers, there are six "vibrations," or types of numbers, that you need to recognize as part of the Pythagorean numerology method. These six are:
1. Life Path
2. Birth Date

3. First Impression
4. Inner Soul
5. Character
6. Expression

Life Path

This is the primary number in Pythagorean Numerology. This information is all about whom you are and your life you are designed to live. It carries the story of your past experiences as well as lifts the veil to lessons you will learn over the course of your life. This is also sometimes referred to as the "Ruling number," "birth path number," or "birth force number." What this number does is reveal the lessons you need to learn in order for you to learn the lessons based on your personal karma. This is why it is considered the primary number in Pythagorean numerology. This number is found in the birthdate of a person. For example, someone born on January 8th, 1985 can calculate their Life Path number by adding the digits together; $1 + 8 + 1 + 9 + 8 + 5 = 32$. The double-digit is not included in the science and therefore needs to be reduced further; $32 = 3 + 2 = 5$. This person's Life Path number is therefore the number five.

Birth Day

During your life, you can use your Birth Day number to shed light on your unique talents, abilities, and personality traits. It also shows you how others view you. This is the simplest calculation in the Pythagorean system. It is simply the number for the day you were born. For example, if a person is born on the 23rd of December, their Birth Day is 23, or $2 + 3 = 5$. Sometimes this number is also called, "Day Number," and "Birth Number."

First Impression

To get this vibration, you add the day and the month of your birth together until you reduce it to a single digit. This is the best number for telling how you first make an impression on someone. When you first talk to a person, you form an opinion of them. This opinion is linked to this number. An example calculation is a person born on January 8th, 1985. They would add their date of birth, 8, to the month or birth, 1. Their First Impression number is 9. For someone born on December 23rd, they would add 23 + 12. The answer, 35, is further reduced to $3 + 5 = 8$, making their First Impression the number 8.

Inner Soul

If you were to rank the numbers of the Pythagorean numerology system, this would be the third most important number for you to know. It is also sometimes called, "Soul's Urge," "Heart's Desire," "Soul's Desire," or "the Vowel's Number." This single number lays bare your deepest desire. It identifies what motivates you and what you want from your life. Sometimes people cannot see this part of who you are, but they can often sense it in you. In order for you to feel that your life is complete and successful, you need to fulfill this deep-set desire. To find this number, you need to take the vowels from your legal name and add them together. You will then reduce that number down to a single digit. This then is your Inner Soul number. For example, the name "Al Pacino" has four vowels, "A" in "Al" and "A," "I," and "O" in "Pacino." "A" is one, "I" is nine, and "O" is 6. This means his Inner Soul equation is 1 + 1 + 9 + 6 = 17 or 1 + 7 = 8.

Character

Again, if you were to rank the numbers in the Pythagorean method, this time you would find this number listed as the least important of them all. This is the number that identifies the "face" you show to the rest of the world. It is the perception that others have of you. It is sometimes also called the "outer personality" number. You find this number by adding the consonant numbers in your legal name. Again, looking at "Al Pacino," the consonants are "L" in "Al," and "P," "C," and "N" in "Pacino." "L" is 3, "P" is 7, and "N" is 5. This makes the Character equation as 3 + 7 + 3 + 5 = 18 and then 1 +8 = 9.

Expression

After Your Life Path number, you need to know your Expression vibration. You use your full legal name to determine this number. Finding this number allows you to find out what you are capable of. It reveals your potential and your strengths as well as defines your destiny. To find this number, add the vowels and consonants together for your name and then reduce them down to a single number. This number reveals your Expression. Again, using "Al Pacino," the vowels equaled 17 and the consonants equaled 18. When you add these two numbers together you get 35. To reduce it further you create the equation, 3 + 5 = 8. It is best to work from the numbers obtained before finding the Character and Inner soul numbers, but you can use them if necessary. For example, the

Character number for "Al Pacino" is 9 and the Inner Soul number is 8. Added together they equal 17, or 1 + 7 = 8.

A Note on Letters

There are nine numbers in the Pythagorean Numerology method. Each letter is assigned a number from one to nine. As you begin the alphabet, each number is given a number until you reach ten. When you would normally count to ten, you would simply start over at one. For example, "A" is one, "B" is two, etc. until you reach "J." "J" returns to one and the count starts over, making "K" two, "L" three, etc. This repeats through the letter "Z".

There are exceptions to the concept of double digits in the Pythagorean system and those are 11 and 22. These are considered "master" numbers and are not reduced to single digits. They are believed to have their own "higher" vibrations. You will learn more about these "master" numbers later on in this book.

CHAPTER 2
Revealing Your Inner Self

Many people go about their daily life without truly learning who they are. They are often confused about the different parts of what makes them unique or their aspects of Self. Many people become trapped in the notion that they are defined by what they do. This means if the things a person does are considered "not good," the person sees themselves as "not good," too. Their actions are what determines their worth to themselves and others. The problem with this is that actions are an external aspect of the Self. Who you are is an internal component? Focusing solely on the external means you never have the opportunity to reveal and embrace the internal side, and therefore never truly tapping into your true self.

Another challenge is when someone considers all three aspects of their Self as one and begins to think they must be "perfect." This perfection can be implied on their Self and also on their actions. What is interesting is that sometimes a person like this applies the need for perfection to negative things, like being "perfect" at an eating disorder, or "perfect" at being sick. If the person feels that they are "perfect" at even these negative things, they feel more worthy and have higher self-esteem. If they feel they are not doing everything, the good and the bad, to the most extreme, they have low self-worth. If you recognize that you fall into one of these two distinctions, it is important for you to understand the three aspects of Self and how each is very distinct and separate from the others. In addition, it is critical that you remove your self-worth, self-esteem, and self-confidence from one aspect of your Self. To help you begin recognizing and defining each aspect, below is a simple breakdown of each;
1. Self-confidence or physical aspect
2. Self-esteem or internal aspect
3. Self-worth or emotional aspect

The first aspect, the aspect of dealing with your physical state of Self, is also tied to your self-confidence. This often accompanies the statement, "I can do _____ well." Or it may feel more like, "I am confident I can do (an activity, task, or behavior) well." If you have lower self-confidence, you may find yourself saying the opposite, or that you cannot do something well. This is an external focus and how your actions result in an emotional response to it. When someone is only tied to their external Self, they can often find themselves waffling between what they feel they do well and what they are lacking and assign that "success" or "failure" to their entire Self. People may view this as attractive behavior at first; a person with low self-confidence may try to improve their performance until they feel they have "perfected" it. These people have ambitious goals and are often determined to accomplish them. The problem with this is that when these goals are not realized, self-confidence and the total sense of Self suffers.

Separating the sense of self-confidence from self-worth and self-esteem is vital for those who suffer from this entanglement. Having low self-confidence in an area does not mean that you are failing at life or are not worthy of great things in your life. For example, you may feel that you are not good at singing, but that does not mean your life is useless. Feeling you are not talented in singing means that you can work on improving your singing abilities if it is important to you, or you can shift your focus to things that you have a higher level of self-confidence in. For example, if you decide to shift from focusing on singing to your ability to play the piano, you can support your higher levels of self-confidence. But again, your ability to play the piano does not determine your self-worth and self-esteem. To help separate self-confidence from the other two aspects, you need to realize that who you are is not the same as what you do.

A person who entangles their whole Self with just self-confidence can end up avoiding risks in life for fear that they will not do it perfectly and they will not be worthy. Instead of diving into perfectionist behavior, they pull back and avoid things in life. If you find you are avoiding something because you are not "perfect" at it or are worried about how it will affect your sense of Self, consider your observation of "who" you are in relation to "what" you do. It is good to risk, practice, and experiment with different things. The more risk you allow yourself to take as you explore various hobbies or interests, the more you boost your self-confidence. The risk is the most important part of developing your self-confidence. This state of being or Self is vulnerable and scary. Trying something new can make you feel exposed or stupid. We often do not give ourselves enough room to practice and learn something new and expect that we will or need to be perfect at anything new we try. This is an unrealistic expectation that often negatively impacts your self-confidence. And if your sense of Self is tied only to your self-confidence, this can be damaging.

Growth comes from risk, practice, and time. You need to allow yourself the time and ability to grow. Instead of focusing on the outcome of an action, consider shifting your perceptions of what you learned from the experience. Instead of asking yourself, "how well did I do this action?" ask yourself, "What did I learn from this experience?" A perception like this can help you push past the fear of failure and take on new risks for growth and improved self-confidence.

The next part of your true Self is your internal perspective or your self-esteem. It is about how you talk to yourself internally based on how you see yourself internally. It is often connected to the other aspects of the Self because it is the relationship you foster with yourself. Sometimes you hear this aspect called your "inner critic." You hear people say that you are often your worst critic or harshest judge. The voice in your head can have a tendency to become negative or disapproving. You can even reject yourself, not accepting your actions or emotions as part of who you are meant to be. The problem with this is that how you treat yourself is vital to how you improve yourself. You improve your self-esteem when you change the tone of your inner "critic" from negative to positive. To determine if you have a positive or negative view of yourself, answer the following:
1. Are you mean to yourself or kind to yourself when you observe your behaviors and actions?
2. Do you reject yourself or accept yourself as you are?
3. Do you show yourself compassion or are you critical of your internal Self and voice?
4. Are you respectful to yourself or do you speak to yourself in a self-demeaning manner?

As you answer these questions, you may or may not be surprised to find that you tend to be more negative to yourself than you are to other people. Sometimes this is because of messages you received as a child. We often hear and interpret messages from childhood and store these "voices" to tell ourselves over and over as we grow. Soon, those messages no longer belong or come from another person, but they are coming from you to yourself. You begin to believe that this messaging is a core part of who you are.

What is important for you to recognize is that you are not the messaging you tell yourself. Your self-esteem is not tied to who you are but rather how you are to yourself. The more positive you are with yourself, the more positive your self-esteem is. The same goes for the negative. It is nice when others think positive thoughts about you, but if you are critical or demeaning to yourself, you will never "believe" them. It is what you believe about yourself that matters. Take time to identify your internal voice and work on rephrasing those internal comments to be positive instead of negative. This will make a dramatic impact on your sense of Self and your self-esteem.

Your self-esteem is internally driven. How you feel about yourself is impacted by external factors, but only you can decide if you are ok and acceptable or not. This means that you have the power to create a new relationship with yourself and change the negative voices from your past. As you foster this new relationship, your self-esteem becomes more positive. You are more accepting, validating and kinder to yourself. You turn from seeking approval in others to seeing yourself as a pillar of strength and positivity.

The third aspect of your Self is your self-worth. This is how you feel you benefit those around you. It is your sense of belonging to the world. It Is directly tied to your interpretation of how well you are accepted and a "part of the tribe." This is related to the physical side of relationships, but also social and spiritual. It is how you know that when you are around you are appreciated but when you are absent you are missed. It can feel closely tied to your heart and gratitude. This sense of Self is not about being approved of by others or making people "like" you, but rather about establishing deep bonds with others on a level often beyond words. This can be a vulnerable place because you are dealing with authenticity rather than seclusion and isolation in relationships. It is developing a connection beyond the surface with something or someone else. There is an inherent risk in this behavior, for fear of rejection. The great relief with a deep connection such as this is that it has the ability to heal past wounds from negative relationships or encounters.

You have three distinct parts to your Self. Each one deals with something specific that makes up who you truly are. Sometimes your Self-changes throughout your life and other times certain traits stick for a length of time or for your lifespan. You can work on different areas of your Self to improve your three aspects individually, bolstering your total Self. This is a valuable tool to have and understand as you learn and apply your numbers revealed in numerology. It is important to recognize that while there are some challenges or different aspects of your life revealed in your numbers, it does not mean you are a "good" or "bad" person. The numbers reveal aspects of your Self that you may or may not already know, and traits you can start to develop early so that problems do not arise later in life.

Your Birth Chart

As mentioned earlier in the first chapter, there are six primary numbers in your birth chart; three are related to your name, and three are related to your birth date. The full birth chart reveals your true Self. It describes what you like and do not like, careers you should pursue the best inner satisfaction, and your expressions to yourself and others. It also reveals insight into your authentic Self that you may not know or ever show to others.

Some of the additional numbers in various forms of numerology include things like cornerstone numbers, hidden talents, karmic lessons, challenge numbers, pinnacle numbers, etc. These are wonderful numbers to explore further, but the foundation of your Self is revealed in your birth chart and illuminated here for you. To help you develop your own birth chart, follow the guidance below:

Record your six numbers here, using the equations outlined in Chapter 1:
    7. Life Path: _____
    8. Birth Date: _____
    9. First Impression: _____
    10. Inner Soul: _____
    11. Character: _____

12. Expression: _____

As a reminder, these numbers are determined by the following equations and information about your life:

- Life Path: Who you are and the lessons you need to learn. Find by adding the month, day, and full year of your birth together until it forms a single number.
- Birth Date: your personality traits and unique abilities. Find by reducing the day of the month of your birth to a single digit. If it is already a single digit, just use that. If it is any number from ten to 31, add the two digits together until they form a single digit. This is the number you should record for your Birth Date.
- First Impression: Learn how others perceive you with this number. It is about first impressions on others. Find this number by adding your birth month number to your day of birth until it forms a single digit.
- Inner Soul: This is the desire that lurks deep in your Soul or heart. It is what you want most from life and what motivates you the most. To find this number you need to use your name and add the numbers associated with all the vowels. Use the Chaldean chart below for numbers to determine this, if necessary.

Number	Letters		
1	A	J	S
2	B	K	T
3	C	L	U
4	D	M	V
5	E	N	W
6	F	O	X
7	G	P	Y
8	H	Q	Z
9	I	R	--

- Character: How you present your Self to others and the rest of the world. Determine this number by adding all the

consonants of your full name together. Use the chart above to help you identify this number, if necessary.
- Expression: Learn what you are capable of accomplishing in life. This is your potential and your strengths. Add all the letters of your full name together and reduce to a single digit.

Now, looking at the numbers in your birth chart, use the words listed below to help you identify what those numbers mean. The numbers identify the flow or course of your life. For example, if your Character number is 5, read the words listed below for the number 5 to understand your character.

1. Egotistical, selfish, dominant, original, starting, independent, masculine, leader
2. Dependent, passive, choice, nurture, empathy, intuitive, cooperative, partner
3. Overbearing, child-like, adaptable, creative, fun, motivated, outspoken
4. Greedy, rebellious, organized, planner, informative, home-focused, teacher or student
5. Irresponsible, dramatic, quick-witted, communicative, active, adventurous, leader, creative
6. An overprotective, smothering, responsible, healthy, guiding light, harmonious, service-oriented, nurturing
7. Anti-social, depressed, independent, questions everything, spiritual, investigative, meditative, psychic
8. Motivated by money, centered on the Self, mature, able to manifest needs and desires, balanced, attracted to the money, business-minded, corporate
9. Aggressive, violent, athletic, cultured, versatile, counselor, completion or endings, humanitarian

In addition, there are two Master numbers that are often not reduced down to single numbers. In addition to knowing the revelations of the Master number, if it appears in your birth chart, you should know the associated single digit for the number, as it often has an influence on the vibrations as well. For example, 11 has its own Master vibration, but it can have influences of 2 in your life, as well.

10. Emotional, sensitive, leader, charismatic, magical, messenger, psychic, illuminated. Also, read about the number 2 listed above.
11. Overly analytical, lazy, idealistic, leader, planner, teacher, business-minded, able to make things happen. Also, read about the number 4 listed above.

The following chart is designed to help you further apply for your numbers in your life and reveal your true Self. The first column, associated with your Birth Date, reveals your gifts. The second column contains a warning about what to overcome or watch out for, and it is related to your Life Path number. The third column shows how you naturally like to express yourself and is related to your Expression number. The final column identifies what is important to you at a deeper level. This is related to your Inner Soul number. Use those numbers to determine your personal reading with the chart below:

1. Birth Date: _____
2. Life Path: _____
3. Expression: _____
4. Inner Soul: _____

Number	Birth Date/ Gifts	Life Path/ Warning	Expression/ Self-expression	Inner Soul/ Importance
1	Original and brave	Selfish	Intelligently	A role as a leader
2	Patient and intuitive	Overly sensitive	Emotionally	Equality and peace
3	Fun and motivated	Extreme	Humorously	Self-expression
4	Practical and unique	Indecisive	Unconventionally	Organization
5	Energetic and witty	Not focused	Through words	Adventures
6	Healing and creative	Judgmental	Creatively	Freedom for creativity

7	Spiritual and psychic	Stand-off-ish	Abstractly	Spiritual connection
8	Business-focused and powerful	Materialistic	With strength	Business
9	Inspirational and competitive	Reliving the past	Passionately	Having something worth fighting for

CHAPTER 3
Individuality Arrows And Their Meaning

The concept of Identity Arrows did not directly appear in the Pythagorean models of numerology; however, it is a clear "pattern" that arises in numerology charts and readings. Pythagoras did identify the occurrence of a "boom" in a chart. These occurrences reveal special features of a person, and when a boom contains a straight line of numbers or empty spaces, there is a special "boom." Booms with a line of numbers reveal a special strength, while a boom with empty boxes reveals a weakness that can be overcome with the other strengths of a person's numbers.

To determine your own arrows, you need to use your Birth Chart, as described in Chapter 2. The numbers are the obvious and major vibrations in your Self, but the arrows are clues to the smaller, and often-unnoticeable traits you possess. You may not readily see these but discovering your arrows can help you find the emotions and traits lying underneath your Self. When you find these out, you can further use this information to help you learn and grow more naturally in your lifetime.

There are four primary types of arrows; the arrow of determination and communication, the arrow of emotion, the arrow of creativity, and the arrow of spirituality.

Determination and Communication

If this arrow is present, you are great at communication. In addition, you are also able to persevere and complete your tasks. You have the organizational ability to pull off incredible tasks and can communicate with others effectively. The best use of this talent is to focus on task completion. Not only do you have a natural tendency for wanting to complete tasks quickly, but you also have the skills, senses, and resources to tackle it. Being able to delegate is a part of this arrow. The way you go about delegating not only helps you easily and quickly accomplish a task, but it also shows your teammates that you are fair and understanding, as well as able to demonstrate how to get the task done.

This arrow shows that you are determined, which if it is not checked, can lead you to be wrapped up in a task and unable to separate from something until you feel it is completed. This determination can end up slowing you down. To help overcome this side effect, learn how to break large tasks into smaller ones and tackle each step one at a time. This way you feel that sense of completion, still working towards the larger goal, but in a more efficient manner. This is a great advantage to have and can help immensely throughout your life.

Emotion

In your everyday life, you have an enhanced ability to recognize and feel your emotions. Not only can you identify how you feel, but you can balance these emotions easily with your intellect. It is easy for you to accept how you feel and find balance when necessary. When you have the ability to recognize and balance in yourself, you can then apply this to others around you. It is almost as if you can see inside of another person, learning how to understand them and their thoughts.

Often your acceptance of your emotions is artistic and creative. You can explore the deeper meaning of how you feel, uncovering what you truly need for comfort and balance, as well as personal insight about yourself. You are intuitive and can see the potential of your emotions. Most of the time you find yourself engaged in developing balance in the outside world. You work towards peace and understanding in others, because you find and honor it in yourself.

In addition to your understanding of emotions, you have an enhanced understanding of the fate and the unconscious mind. The challenge with this arrow is that others do not see or understand emotions as you do. You have a keen understanding of the senses that not many embody. Your emotional reactions may also be very different than others because you understand your emotions and fate better than others. Having deeper feelings than others is often a challenge as well. You may need to find ways to protect your Self from the intense emotions every now and then. It is a great tool when managed because you intuitively understand your emotions and those of the people around you.

Creativity

A creative arrow not only identifies your ability to be creative but also our intellectual ability. You can visualize and also apply your vision. Often you find yourself drawn to humanitarian concepts or principles and can easily see how you can help. You are idealistic. You have integrity. Sometimes you can become too attached to your own ideas, which requires you to learn how to listen to others and accept ideas from others as well.

The amazing thing about this arrow is not just your ideas, but your ability to turn an idea into reality. You are fully capable of seeing how you can manifest concepts and principles in reality. Although you are capable of this, you need to learn how to get to this point. This may take practice and work to reach this high point, but once you do you will be extraordinary!

Unlike many others, your ability to communicate, especially through creative outlets, is unique. Your judgment is often correct because you balance your creativity with reason. Throughout your life, you will enjoy creativity and intellectual skills. Whenever you need to find a solution that is "outside the box," you will have no problem identifying new ways to do something.

Spirituality

A person with a spiritual arrow is compassionate. They are also very aware of spiritually. Most of your life you see things from a spiritual point of view. Almost any activity you undertake your approach with a spiritual outlook, including your daily activities. You find comfort and joy in self-reflection, time to yourself, and learning more about life's mysteries. There is a strong desire for you to serve others. You are naturally genuine and caring. You seek to help others in your normal, daily interactions. Every person you encounter immediately senses your compassion and caring inside of you. It does not matter how you are feeling or what you are doing, people sense this serenity and nurturing inside of you.

Throughout your life, your spirituality helps you be at peace and aware of God's presence. It is especially helpful for times of stress or hardship. You can rely on this arrow when you need to make a decision and it helps you slow down and reflect what decision really needs to be made.

In addition to these different arrows, there are arrows that are generally associated with strengths or weaknesses. As mentioned in the beginning, having an "absent" arrow, or numbers missing from a series, indicate a weakness, while having certain numbers in a sequence often identifies a strength. It is important to note that just because something is labeled as a "strength" or "weakness" does not mean it is guaranteed to work well for a person. Often, they are merely an illumination of skill or trait that is deep inside you that will get better with attention and development.

When you understand a trait that you have or a "weakness" that can hold you back from your true potential, you now have the ability to make the most of what your life has to offer.

Strength arrows are when three very specific numbers are aligned in a specific pattern. This pattern appears diagonally, horizontally, or vertically. Below are some of the arrow orientations and numbers that signify the strength:

1, 5, and 9 diagonal: Arrow of Determination
- Sometimes the number 4 is present in a person's chart to balance this arrow. If number 4 is absent, this person probably will have an intense temper.

3, 5, and 7 diagonal: Arrow of Compassion
- All people born with an arrow of compassion in the 20th century also have an arrow of determination. This arrow is also sometimes called the arrow of Mysticism.

3, 6, and 9 horizontal: Arrow of Intellect

2, 5, and 8 horizontal: Arrow of Emotion or Emotional Balance

1, 4, and 7 horizontal: Arrow of Practicality

3, 2, and 1 vertical: Arrow of Emotional Balance
- These need to appear in the first column of your grid for this arrow to appear.

4, 5, and 6 vertical: *Arrow of Willpower*
- These need to appear in the middle column of your grid for this arrow to appear. This is very rare and uncommon. This is an arrow of uncompromising endurance, courage, and strength.

9, 8, and 7 vertical: *Arrow of Activity*
- These need to appear in the third column of your grid for this arrow to appear.

Missing numbers from your grid in a certain pattern identify an arrow of weakness. Like arrows of strength, certain patterns show a specific trait of a person that needs to be developed. In the instance of a missing number, or an arrow of weakness, you need to exert extra effort to bring change into this area. These arrows are wonderful places for people to start on their path to self-development as they are clear opportunity revealed to them in their numbers.

Below are some of the arrow orientations and numbers that signify the weakness:

1, 5, and 9 missing from a chart, three spaces in a line: *Arrow of Indecision*
- This is very rare and not seen in the mast millennia; however, people will begin to exhibit this arrow now. These people may appear likable and caring; however, they struggle to make a decision that would not please all people.

3, 5, and 7 missing from a chart, spaces near each number: *Arrow of Skepticism*
- Things must be demonstrated or shown before acceptance. Trust is lacking.

3, 6, and 9 missing from a chart: *Arrow of Poor Memory*
- No one born in the 20th century could have this arrow, but it is possible now for those born in the 21st. This does not mean a person is incapable of being intellectual or have a good memory, it indicates that people will need to develop skills to support these areas.

2, 5, and 8 missing from a chart: Arrow of Emotional Sensitivity

1, 4, and 7 missing from a chart: Arrow of Impracticality

- There has been no evidence of someone having this arrow in the last thousand years, but those born in the last decade may exhibit this arrow.

4, 5, and 6 missing from a chart, running vertically through the center of the chart: Arrow of Frustration

- This often indicates a person's expectation from others that is unrealistic.

7, 8, and 9 missing from a chart: Arrow of Hesitation

- No one born in the 20th century has this arrow because of the presence of the number 9; however, those born in the 21st and beyond can have this arrow.

In addition to the arrows, when a number appears more than one time, there is a special meaning behind it. The following list defines what each number means, including when it appears two or more times in your chart:

Number 1

When this number only appears once in a chart, people may find it challenging to express their feelings or desires. While they may not be bad at communication in general, it is isolated to communicating their feelings or on other levels. It can also reveal a challenge in appreciating alternative points of view. Two one's in a chart is much more balanced. Expression of feelings and desires is easier. These people often have a more unbiased outlook on life and can judge other's views more effectively. This is the best number of ones to have in your chart.

After the second one, the following repetitions begin to split a person's personality. Three ones, for example, create a person who can talk and be outgoing sometimes or quiet and reserved at other times. It depends on the situation. When a person has four one's they have a hard time expressing their feelings, leading to a lot of misunderstandings. They struggle with letting things go and relaxing, especially around groups of people. Those with five to seven one's means there is a stark inability to verbally express yourself. This creates incredible challenges in your life, including constant misunderstanding. To compensate for this, many find expression through creative outlets instead of words. This overabundance of one's can also indicate someone who tends to over-indulge in various areas.

Number 2

The following list identifies the traits one or more of a number can reveal in your chart:

1. Intuitive and sensitive. Easily hurt. Can see through other's insincerity and are a good judge of others.
2. Very sensitive and intelligent. Outstanding intuition and benefits greatly from this ability. Master at detecting and assessing the intentions of others.
3. Social situations are often loathsome and are avoided for fear of being hurt. People with this many two's in their chart can be overly sensitive and live in their own world. Others may view this person as aloof. In addition, a person with three 2's may have premonitions.
4. Overreacting to small issues is related to four 2's and the rash and impatient nature of these people. Like those with three 2's, these people tend to stay to themselves for fear of being hurt.
5. This is a rare occurrence. People with five 2's are often incredibly sensitive and have trouble dealing with themselves and the rest of the world around them. They lack self-confidence and trust.

Number 3

1. Creative and good memory. Positive and practical. Attain goals honestly and realistically. Often very optimistic and inspires others.
2. Creative as well, but more mentally aware. A little "crazy" or eccentric makes them more unconventional than others. Great at verbal expression.
3. Overly-imaginative and often live in their own "world." Self-absorbed, remote, and aloof. Often bad listeners and have trouble relating to others. Sometimes petty and argumentative, although very intelligent.

4. Very rare to find. Overly-dreamy, fearful, timid, or impractical. Imagination is so strong that it leads to an inability to live in the real world with real routines.

Number 4

  1. Great with more physical or manual work. Well-grounded and practical. Careers that are more hands-on are best. Great at the organization.
  2. Also great at organization. The ability to tackle a hands-on project and see it through to the end. Very proper, conscientious and accurate. Sometimes more involved in materialistic endeavors than spiritual ones.
  3. Almost exclusive physical actions. The organization is almost compulsive or maniacal. Works hard and is self-disciplined. Sometimes it is hard to see their own abilities and can end up working in a career that is not the best fit for their skills.
  4. Again, very rare. Only interested in and engaged in physical activities. If asked to engage in something intellectual or spiritual, this person is not interested or capable of grasping.

Number 5

  1. Balanced and stable in their emotions. Can inspire and motivate others. Caring and compassionate.
  2. Determined, emotional, and intense. Driven and enthusiastic. Passionate, sometimes to the point of obsession. Can have trouble holding in all the emotions, leading to outbursts.
  3. A risk-taking streak, limitless energy, and unwavering drive. Love adventure and excitement. Speaks without thinking. Enjoys change.
  4. Has only happened in 3% of the population over the last 100 years. Dangerous to have this combination. Accident prone and contemplation is necessary before taking any action.

Number 6

  1. Love in the home and with friends and family. Excellent parents and children. Love household affairs. Creative. When things go wrong, friends and family turn to this person. Can be insecure and worried for others.
  2. Overly anxious, especially over family and close friends. Need to relax more than others. Love beautiful things around them. Overly protective.

3. Overprotective and possessive of those that they love, leading to creating a dependency in their children. Often negative and restless. Incredibly creative.
4. Driven and creative. Emotionally vulnerable and weak. Life is difficult to handle.

Number 7
1. Learns lessons through the loss of health, possessions, or love. Each lesson enhances its maturity and pursuits.
2. Very analytical and good at solving complex problems. Each loss leads to more interest and passion in the spiritual realm.
3. Silent and strong. Sad in life. Setbacks and losses negatively impact their lives. Inner reserves of strength often develop during their life.
4. This is the unluckiest combination of numbers. Fate uses them to teach lessons of life. It is also very rare.

Number 8
1. Detailed, fastidious, and methodical. The active and restless mind. Desires constant mental challenge. Have trouble finishing tasks.
2. Observant and perceptive. Learn through experience. Does not trust others as a reference. Can be inflexible and has trouble changing plans.
3. Restless and rigid. Materialistic and a perfectionist.
4. Love change and constantly changes patterns and routines. Must find their true purpose and are restless until then.

Number 9
1. Constantly working to improve the Self. Ambitious. All people have at least one 9.
2. Astute, intelligent, and idealistic. Can be critical of others. Derogatory and blunt at times. Can look down on others.
3. Brilliant and virtuous. Maturity improves this person and their life. Can exaggerate and be more negative.
4. 4 /5. Gifted with intelligence. Vulnerable to mundane daily situations. Only people born on 9/9/1999, 9/19/1999, or 9/29/1999 have this rare combination. The next occurrence will not happen again until 2999.

CHAPTER 4
Ruling And Day Numbers

The Ruling number is also called your Birth Date. It is the day of your birth, reduced to a single digit. For example, if you are born on the 12th, you would add 1 + 2 = 3. This number identifies a person's personality. It also provides insight into your positive and negative traits. Because of this, this number has a tremendous impact on your life.

If you are working on your relationship or want to know about your compatibility with another person, use both your ruling number and theirs. Your ruling number can also be used for determining the best career fit for you, based on your natural tendencies. Many times, you can also use your ruling number to identify common health concerns you may have or could develop. In addition, your Ruling number shares what is "lucky" for you. This includes days that are lucky, stones, and even colors.

Ruling numbers, like much of numerology, is influenced or impacted by astrology as well. Many people will adjust the reading of their Ruling number based on celestial bodies, such as the alignment of planets or stars. The influence of the planets or other celestial bodies is used to predict how certain events will play out for a person.

Most predictions made in your numerology chart are based on this number. For those using astrology alongside numerology for understanding who you are and what will be happening, the Ruling number is used, along with the position as related to the associated celestial body. For example, if your ruling number is 3, you would use the positioning of Jupiter, the planet associated with the number 3, to determine how you will "do" in a certain situation. Most of the time, a person with a Ruling number of 3 is hardworking and moral. They are imaginative and idealists. They are also less materialistic, often opting for a simpler life and possessions.

The more detailed reading or chart you can get, the more understanding you can discover about yourself. Your Ruling number identifies the underlying influences in your life; the values that guide your decisions and happiness. It can also shed light on your destiny and how you can decide what path is best for you. This is why many people use this information for their career path. For those that are more intellectual, and fewer hands-on, a career in construction or mechanics may be less fulfilling than a role as a professor or entrepreneur. And vice versa! Even when you align your career path with your Ruling number you are not going to be without obstacles. The great benefit is that you now understand your unique identity and how you can overcome these obstacles for the best opportunity for success in life.

Below is a list of what your Ruling number can mean in your life:

Number 1
Your day of birth is the 1st, 10th, 19th, or the 28th
- Organized
- Efficient
- Great as leaders and managers

Number 2
Your day of birth is 2nd, 11th (occasionally, as this is a Master Number), 20th, or the 29th
- Balanced
- Cooperative
- Sensitive
- Harmony at all times is important

Number 3
Your day of birth is either the 3rd, 12th, 21st, or the 30th
- Emotional
- Wise
- Intellectual
- Dedicate to the wellbeing of others
- Works to make a change

Number 4
Your day of birth is the 4th, 13th, 22nd (occasionally, as this is a Master Number), or the 31st
- Organized
- Detail oriented

- Hard worker
- Determined to accomplish tasks
- Let's go of personal desires to accomplish professional goals

Number 5
Your day of birth is the 5th, 14th, or the 23rd
- Hard working
- Shrewd
- Entertaining
- Balanced
- Cheerful, even when challenged

Number 6
Your day of birth is the 6th, 15th, or the 24th
- Beautiful
- Aesthetic
- Peaceful
- Creative and thrives in a creative career

Number 7
The day of your birth is the 7th, 16th, or the 25th
- Intelligent
- Knowledgeable
- Wise
- Drawn to education
- Destined to accomplish a lot of great things in life

Number 8
The day of your birth is the 8th, 17th, or 26th
- Courageous
- Hard working
- Nurturing
- Focused on providing for your family
- Desires a close family unit

Number 9
The day of your birth is the 9th, 18th or the 27th
- Generous
- Romantic
- Humanitarian
- Very social

Personal Day Numbers

Also similar to astrology, you can use numerology to help predict how a specific day will resonate in the future. You probably already recognize how some days tend to be more dramatic than others, or that you seem "off" on some days for no apparent reason. You often hear the phrase, "work up on the wrong side of the bed." For those that follow numerology, you can help identify the "tone" or vibration of a day, which then reveals how that day will typically flow. Understanding this can then help you know how you will be affected and what, if anything, you can do about it.

Use this information on a daily basis to learn how your flow of life will be on any day in your future. There are a few reasons why it is beneficial to know this. It is possible to gain an advantage in life, first and foremost. Using this information allows you to enjoy more certainty in your day. Of course, these tones are not predictions, but the tone or track of the day can be shown. You can use this knowledge to determine if it will align with your plans for that day and how to approach the day accordingly. It is a definite edge.

The calculations are slightly more challenging for determining your personal numbers; however, there are several online calendar generators. For example, enter your name and birthdate into this calendar generator, https://affinitynumerology.com/numerology-tools/personal-day-calendar.php, and it will assign personal numbers from one to nine for every day during a certain month. You can then use those numbers to determine the day's tone.

Once you know your personal numbers, you can then use the following guide to help you define the tendency of the day:

Personal Number 1: Great for planning projects. Undertake a procedure or project that is connected to self-determination or self-sufficiency. Independence is important for this day.

Personal Number 2: Focus on your relationships. This is a good day for teamwork, considering other people's feelings, and be a peacemaker. This day also tends to be diplomatic and tactful, especially in relation to issues.

Personal Number 3: Creativity and personal expression rules this day. Interacting socially is also common and attached to your creativity. This is also an optimistic day.

Personal Number 4: Accomplish your tasks methodically today for the best success. This is also a day that is a secure foundation for the future.

Personal Number 5: Personal freedom is the energy for a day with this number. During this day you will often be interested in one thing after another. It is also a day where you may easily see multiple viewpoints.

Personal Number 6: Today is a day for family and the home. It is supportive and nurturing. This can extend beyond the family to your community and the activities outside your home as well.

The Personal Number 7: Look inside for the answers on this day. It is important to exercise introspection. Today you can solve problems and gain wisdom. This is a good day for looking into spiritual and scientific matters for better understanding and intuition.

Personal Number 8: Gather material needs and improve finances on this day. The energy on a day with this number is all about business. You build long-term value on days with this number. This is also a pragmatic and efficient day.

Personal Number 9: The energy of this day is about the welfare of your community or the world. Use your imagination and creative thoughts. You may feel a strong urge to do something important or meaningful for your community or humanity on this day.

Personal Number 11: This Master Number is very spiritual. It has the energy of peace, harmony, charisma, and intuition. A day with this number tends to focus on teaching and spiritual relationships. This also typically embodies the energy of the number 2, as well.

The Personal Number 22: Another Master Number is the energy of 22. This vibration is about bringing forward the spiritual and social benefits. You can easily encourage others to work together to find a solution to a common issue. This is about self-confidence, practicality, and methodical intentions. This also typically embodies the energy of the number 4, as well.

CHAPTER 5
Your Peak And Pinnacle Years

Throughout your life, there are four cycles that are important to your life's journey. These peak years, or pinnacle years, illustrate a specific lesson you are developing during that time. You need to know your Life Path number and from there you can determine the length or each phase. Typically, the first pinnacle lasts from your birth through to your age of 27 through 35. This depends on your Life Path. The next pinnacle lasts for nine years, and the last goes through the end of your life. These are the three phases, peaks, or pinnacles of your life.

When you transition from one pinnacle to the next you feel a dramatic shift in your life. When you move into the next phase you will encounter new events and situations, and you will also experience challenges and a new atmosphere. To help you prepare for these changes and these years, you should know your pinnacle years and what the numbers say. Once you know when you are going to transition into a new peak year, it is important that you begin preparing for the move as early as possible, ideally two years in advance. As your preparations come to an end, at the end of the two years and just before the change into a new pinnacle year, the decisions you make will alter your life. This includes marriages, career changes, and other alterations to your character. Typically, the strongest transition occurs between the first and second phase of life. It is also usually the most difficult. The great thing about crossing this path is that you see a more direction you will sense on your journey. You also grasp more about who you are. This transition is all about becoming more mature.

As mentioned before, the dates of your peak years are based on your Life Path number. Below is a chart to help you use this to define your age in each pinnacle:

Life	*1st Pinnacle*	*2nd Pinnacle*	*3rd Pinnacle*
1	0-35	36-45	46+
2	0-34	35-44	45+
3	0-33	34-43	44+

4	0-32	33-42	43+
5	0-31	32-41	42+
6	0-30	31-40	41+
7	0-29	30-39	40+
8	0-28	29-38	39+
9	0-27	28-37	38+
11	0-34	35-44	45+
22	0-32	33-42	43+

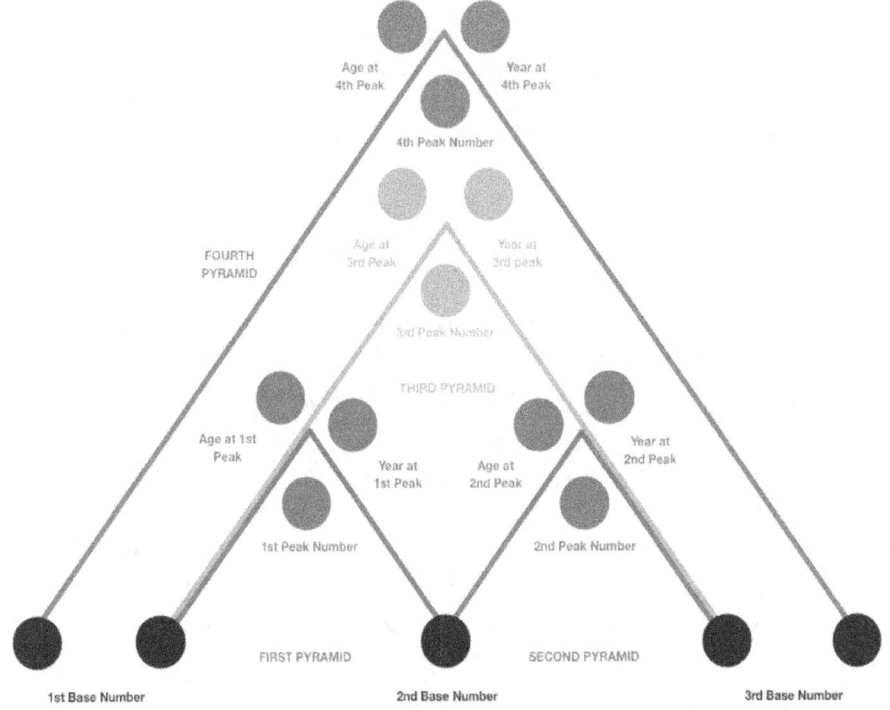

The following equations are used to define your pinnacle numbers:

1st Pinnacle: month plus your date of birth. For example, someone born on 5/17 would have the first pinnacle number of 4.

2nd Pinnacle: Date of your birth plus the year. For example, if the person born on 5/17 was born in 2000, their second pinnacle number is 8.

3rd Pinnacle: Add the first pinnacle number to the second pinnacle number. In the running example, this means 4 + 8 = 12 or 1+ 2 = 3.

Now that you know about your pinnacle years, it is important to find your own Personal Year. This helps in determining the course of the upcoming year before you. It lays out the clues for what lays ahead. To begin finding your personal year number, use the date and month of your year. Reduce this number down to a single digit. While normally you do not reduce a Master Number down to a single digit, in this instance you will want to reduce the number 11 and 22 to 2 and 4. For example, if your birthday is May 3rd, your number would be 5 + 3 = 8.

After, take the current year or the year that you are looking to review and reduce it to a single digit. For example, if you are looking to determine your Personal Year number for 2025, you would add all the numbers together. In this example, the equation would look like 2 + 2 + 5 = 9. Now, add the year digit to your month and date number, and reduce to a single digit. In the current example, add 8 + 9 = 17, or 1+ 7 = 8. This means that in 2025, your personal year is 8. This number shares with you the traits or tone for the whole year for you. Once you determine your personal year, use the outline below for determining the tone of your year:

Personal Year 1: Your Life's New Beginning

A Personal Year number 1 reveals the start of a new nine-year cycle. This year is one of promise and exciting adventure. There will be new challenges that create a way for the next nine years. When you experience a Personal Year 1, take the time to become clear about what you want to accomplish and then go after them. It often requires a lot of hard work to make this happen, but this is also why you have a surge in personal strength at this time. You need this extra energy to make things happen. If for any reason, you decide to resist the changes coming, you risk delaying the developments for another nine years. Do not focus on the past, but rather stay focused on the new goals and tasks ahead of you. Set to the work at hand and let go of what came before. Most of the time this is easy for those entering a Personal Year 1. The past often holds a host of disappointments and issues that you will be willing to let fade into the past. This is a wonderful year, so soak it all up!

Personal Year 2: Patience, collaboration and improvement

Unlike a Personal Year 1 intended for action and change, this is a year of patience and observation. You will be a background character, often working more on yourself than on the external factors around you. This is a time of growth, especially personal. Do not try to force problems or forward momentum. Instead, look for relationships and teamwork. These will benefit you later on, and now is the time to foster them. It is like you are collecting things for the future actions you will need to take. Collet relationships and traits that will serve you in your upcoming transitions. Because of the patience required to develop and foster relationships and personal growth, you should avoid being too aggressive in situations. Expect stops, detours, and delays to occur during this time. It is also a time of small contributions and attending to details. Maybe you focus on helping another person and their goals. For some, a year like this is a test of emotional and self-control. If you have worked solo before, working as a team may be hard at first. Try to develop a sense of calm and collection. It is common to fall into a state of depression and can sometimes cause a level of anxiety or tension. Be prepared and aware of this tendency. On the other hand, Personal Year 2 is a great time to support or create deep relationships. It is also a great year to get married. If you are already married, this is a great year to strengthen your relationship.

Personal Year 3: Creativity and a social circle

What a happy and social year! The vibration of this year is cheerful and bright. Check in with old friends and make new ones. Allow your romance to bloom and grow. This is a year to embrace your life's path fully, even if it means you will have to face consequences for your choices later on. This is not the year to experience consequences, so take advantage. Just remember, you will face them eventually. While you will still have responsibilities, the restrictions of these will seem less. Be careful not to spread yourself too thin or take on too much at once. Instead, take a bit of time to just pamper yourself while still keeping your goals in sight. Do not let the temptation of complete bliss derail your ultimate plans. Verbal and artistic skills are easily developed during this year, so give yourself time to foster such endeavors.

This is a happy year personally, but professionally it can be a challenge. Your attitude is often perceived as frivolous and scattered. Your attitude can lead to a rash and impractical environment. You can leave tasks unfinished. Your finances may suffer because of this or other frivolous factors of a year like this. Thankfully, you can expect a balance in the following year.

Personal Year 4: Slow and steady wins the race

Your hard work during this year will be the balance to the happy frivolity you had in a Personal Year 3. You have goals and tasks that need to be accomplished and now is the time to do it. You need to dig in your heels, exercise good self-discipline, and get things done. It can be frustrating, especially when you put forth a great deal of effort and it does not produce the dramatic results you desire. It can feel like you are taking "one step forward and two steps back" constantly throughout this year. Instead of being frustrated by the current situation, take time to look at the past and the present and get organized for the culture. Be clear about it all, and shine light into all the dark corners of your past experiences. The previous year was high-flying, but this year is very down-to-earth. You will notice your expectations and responsibilities increase during this year in response to your hard work and efforts. This is a good year to look into your diet and overall health. This is especially important because your physical self is compromised and you may often come down with some illness or another. Take a bit of time to tidy up your affairs and get ready for the next, hectic year coming up.

Personal Year 5: Playing it fast, free, and loose

Get ready for some big changes! Your growth is not limited and your opportunities expand. This includes making new friends and engaging in more social activities. More than years past, expect adventure and excitement. You can shake free from the old routines that no longer serve you and be free to chart a new direction. The last year can be challenging and seem to stifle your freedom, but this year you can be loose. Unfortunately, with all this freedom and opportunity you can seem a little scattered. You may have trouble focusing on the little details. Not being able to do the little things like you used to can feel very limiting and even boxed in. However, if you approach it with understanding and appreciation, you can enjoy a free and exciting year that brings in big changes to all areas of your life.

Personal Year 6: Take responsibility at home, with your family, and in love

Your concern and nurturing over your family and loved ones increase this year. You may bring on more responsibility, or just focus more on those around you more. Often this is a year where you will need to make a sacrifice for those close to you, causing changes to your own personal life. Do not expect to make major alterations to your life this year. Instead, focus on making adjustments to your goals based on the needs of this year. Also, work on finishing projects you started before. This year your efforts may not bound forward like years past, but they will grow and move. Expect to see beautiful developments in your relationships at home, work, and love. It will be easy for you to foster an emotional connection with those close to you, and they in return will be more emotionally open to you as well. Accept that this year will be at a slower pace than the past and take time to enjoy the harmony and tranquility this year brings.

Personal Year 7: Understand your analysis

Take a moment, this year to be exact, to pause in your activities, and reflect. Look inside of you and discover how your goals and path are progressing. You have been surrounded by very active and fast-paced years, but this year is a time for reflection. It is time to learn about yourself and bring an understanding of light. You will spend a lot of time focused on yourself and often seek quiet and private time to be alone and think. You will also seek to avoid responsibility as much as possible in these situations. This includes removing yourself from pressures of business. Instead of pushing forward with goals and plans, like years before, take the time to look back to the past to learn and look at the future for planning purposes. You may not accomplish a lot of external achievements, but you will develop internally. It is a great year to spend studying and writing. The act of writing will help you integrate your thoughts, analyze what you are learning, and study the content more deeply. Your intellect is piqued during this year and you can take full advantage of this desire to learn and understand. Your personality may appear aloof and detached from situations and others during this year. Do not allow your relationships to suffer, but your attention is best focused on developing your skills for later use. Pursue additional education, or find time to enhance your meditation practice for internal reflection.

Personal Year 8: Gain and attain

What a powerful year to transition into! This is a year of great accomplishment. After finishing an introspective and calm year, this is a time for ambition. It is time to use the skills you developed in the last year. Make big, life-changing decisions and accomplish great things. You will be occupied, involved, and active. Your work will no longer be passive, but current and consistent. You have the opportunity to do great things with the work in front of you, so take full advantage and go after it. In business, allow yourself to get outside of your boundaries and expand. Allow your self-confidence and authority to shine this year. Others will see and appreciate your leadership and ownership over your actions. This is the peak of your status and power in your life during this nine-year cycle, especially right at the end of the year, before transitioning into your Personal Year 9.

Personal Year 9: Reflect and also reach out

This ninth year is an interesting one. You are wrapping up loose ends, taking inventory of various parts of your life, and reflecting on what you are proud of and what you would like to bring a big change to. It is not necessarily a time for reflecting on things like ideals and values, or revisiting things that were once important to you, but rather looking at your actions and achievements. This year is also a year to reach out and help others. It is a year for giving to others and not just focusing on yourself. This year is closely connected to the Earth and nature, and you may feel more drawn to it this year than in other years past. Part of this is the feeling of escape or release you are feeling. You have a lot of things you have been working on the past nine years, and this is a time for it to come to an end. You should close out any last details to prepare for the year of new that is about to begin, starting your next nine-year cycle.

CHAPTER 6
Connections Between Astrology And Numerology

There is a dance between numerology and astrology. While they are two different entities; one being the study of numbers and the other on the movement of the planets, there are overlaps. For example, both turn to your birth date to gather information about your future. Astrology looks to the alignment of the planets during the time of your birth while numerology looks to the numbers associated with your birth. It sometimes appears to be two very different topics, but in truth the two are linked. And when you use the two together, they become a powerful combination. The two together reveal incredible insights into the meaning and direction of your life.

Astrology, to begin, uses numbers in a lot of different ways. Geometry is necessary to figure out the calculations of the planets. The degrees and angles are also important in astrology. To find someone's birth chart in astrology, numbers are essential. Numbers appear throughout astrology on a regular basis. What is interesting is that while astrology needs numbers, numerology does not need any aspect of astrology for understanding. But while it is not necessary, it is helpful. The information provided through numerology is enhanced with the understanding and application of astrology.

To begin, one of the closest connections between astrology and numerology is the link between the numbers 0-9 and the planets. Each planet is assigned a number from zero through nine. These include both the sun and the moon, as well. These are important numbers in numerology. Astrology is a much more complex method for predicting and understanding life, meaning numerology is easier to grasp and master than later.

When both were developed, around the same time as one another, the science of astrology and numerology were some of the most accurate methods for understanding life and preparing for the future. While today both are considered "new age" and are often dismissed as esoteric "silliness," as anyone who has experienced reading from a professional practitioner, the accurate evidence helps reveal the relevant science behind the two. There are common themes and similarities between an astrological and numerology reading. The subjects and methods for determining the reading are independent and unique of one another, yet the connection to the energy of the Universe is made clear in the related information shared between the readings. Keep in mind that the practice of assigning a masculine or feminine tone is used in both numerology and astrology. Below is a chart that defines the numbers associated with each astrological sign, as well as what gender each number and sign is assigned:

Number	Astrological Sign	Gender
1	Aries	Masculine
2	Taurus	Feminine
3	Gemini	Masculine
4	Cancer	Feminine
5	Leo	Masculine
6	Virgo	Feminine
7	Libra	Masculine
8	Scorpio	Feminine
9	Sagittarius	Masculine
10	Capricorn	Feminine
11	Aquarius	Masculine
12	Pisces	Feminine

If you notice the pattern, all the odd numbers, which also correspond with either fire or air signs are masculine. On the other hand, the even numbers are feminine and include all the earth and water astrological signs. The energy contained in these numbers and signs are the primary energies of the Universe. Furthermore, while each energy is unique and dominant none or another, there is evidence of both energies in every sign and number.

There are obvious compliments to each science; numerology and astrology. When you learn more about both you can enhance your understanding of yourself and the world around you. Each one provides clarity and understanding, but together you can open more doors to aspects of your Self and the Universe you did not know before. You have special gifts designed to be shared with the rest of humankind, but sometimes these gifts lie hidden or stifled inside of you. There is meaning behind what happens to you, and as you master the art of numerology, and bring in the science of astrology, you can tap into the Universal knowledge and learn so much. It is not exploration for the mundane or average person. Learning the ancient mystics is deep and personal. You are a blessed member of a spiritual community few dares to explore.

While this book is primarily about numerology and the practice, for the purpose of shedding light on the connection between it and astrology, a brief introduction and outline of astrology are further provided for your understanding. During this introduction, if your interest is piqued in astrology, you should continue your research further. The more you understand of the two sciences, the more detailed and clear you can become. For now, reference below for an introduction.

An Overview of Astrology

A long time ago humankind looked to the sky in wonderment at the stars and planets. It seems natural to think that the movement of the sky was like magic to these early ancestors. It is also natural to recognize that these people recorded their observations of the movement in the sky. A record or journal by the Greek historian, Solon, reveals that nine thousand years before he was born people were observing and recording their observations of the sky, stars, and planets. This is perhaps the earliest mention of astrological study, meaning people have been studying and recording our atmospheric movements for about 11 thousand years. This makes it one of the oldest forms of divine or spiritual study in the world.

The origin of astrology is unknown. Many people identify Mesopotamia as the birthplace of astrology; however, there is evidence that forms of this study have occurred in Egypt, Babylon, Greece, and China. These early astronomers identified the constellations, or grouping of certain stars, and how they traversed the sky as a single unit, while the brightest five stars, which are larger than the others, appeared to wander on their own paths. Because of this independent movement, the earliest astrologers named these stars the "wanderers." The name you use for them today is "planets." Because of their unique and independent nature, the ancient ancestors considered these stars gods and gave them special names, such as Mercury, Venus, Mars, Jupiter, and Saturn. These are the five planets more easily viewable from Earth. Later Uranus was discovered, in 1781, and Neptune in 1846. Pluto was identified in 1930, and later debate has emerged about its assignment as a planet, dwarf planet, or another astrological item. In addition to monitoring the planets and stars, these ancestors also recorded the movements of the moon and sun. This information is a powerful tool in the science of astrology.

Over time, those studying this information observed that the birth of a person correlated to the position of the planets, sun and moon in the sky, and those with similar correlations tended to be similar to one another. It is and has always been obvious that each person is a unique soul, but some personality and natural tendencies run as a common thread amongst some, such as a similar approach to interests and feelings. Once this connection was identified, astrologers began developing the charts for horoscopes to help individuals learn more about their true Self. A "horoscope" is actually an image of the sky during the place, time, and date of that person's birth. For example, if you could see the sky the moment you were born, possible through a telescope, you would be able to see the alignment of the planets, sun, and moon the minute you came into this world.

When this was first identified the preparation of a horoscope chart was a time consuming and long process. Astrologers would reference and calculate to find just the right information about who you were based on that astronomical information. Now, this information is available at your fingertips, just seconds away! A simple "Google" for a horoscope chart will reveal hundreds of different sites offering this information to you for free. But while you can get access to this information, it is important to recognize that interpreting and understanding this information can take years to unravel and comprehend.

How the Four Elements Come into Play

Each of the 12 zodiac signs is assigned an element, meaning each one falls into one of four categories. Empedocles, the Greek philosopher, was the first to assign an element to the four categories of astrological signs. This occurred about 2,500 years ago and has stuck ever since. This is because the elements are the foundation of the Earth as well as the entire Universe. The four together reveal the essential truth of the various astrological signs. The four elements are water, air, earth, and fire.

Water: The astrological signs for water are Pisces, Scorpio, and Cancer. A person with this element is often spiritual, intuitive, creative, emotional, understanding, forgiving, and compassionate.

Air: The astrological signs for water are Aquarius, Libra, and Gemini. A person with this element is often trusting, intellectual, entertaining, impractical, communicative, independent, restless, curious, joyful. And lighthearted.

Earth: The astrological signs for water are Capricorn, Virgo, and Taurus. A person with this element is often persevering, solid, dependable, disciplined, focused, practical, ambitious, reliable, responsible, and cautious.

Fire: The astrological signs for water are Sagittarius, Leo, and Aries. A person with this element is often initiating, passionate, powerful, courageous, inspirational, impulsive, enthusiastic, energetic, assertive, and positive.

How the Sun Affects the Signs

The entire solar system is powered by the strength and energy of the sun. Without it, nothing could or would exist. Sun, in the context of your horoscope, is identified as popularity, creativity, motivation, leadership, energy, strength, willpower, or independence. It is also the force behind who you are or your true Self. It is what makes you unique.

Even if you know nothing about your horoscope chart, chances are you know your Sun sign. And chances are you know a little bit about what character traits are assigned to your Sun sign. The predictions and outlines in magazines and newspapers are based on your Sun sign. Rightfully so, these are general predictions. There are 12 Sun signs, and every person falls under one sign. Of course, not everyone is perfectly fit into one generalization, but it is a nice and easy place to start as you begin to understand your astrological horoscope chart.

The zodiac signs, all 12 of them, have a specific part of the sky. If you were to look at an astrological map of the sky, you would see that there are 12 distinct sections, one of each of the zodiacs. It is somewhat even, and each piece looks like a slice from a circle cake. When you were born the Sun was in situated inside one of these Zodiac slices, determining your Sun sign. The Sun rotates around the sky and spends about 30 days in each zodiac wedge. This is why it takes the Sun a full year to circle around the zodiac chart.

Every year or so the exact dates of the zodiac change because of this cycle. This means that if you were born close to the "edge" of the zodiac, you should not just assume you are the zodiac sign listed for this current year. It would benefit you to look at the Sun position from the year you were born to find out your birth Sun sign. In addition, those born on the "edges" of a sign tend to embody some of the traits of the next closest sign to them, as well as their birth Sun sign. Previously, a common assumption was that those born on the fringes of a sign, and that embodied two zodiacs, only received the positive traits of each sign and were spared the more negative aspects. While this is not necessarily true or accurate, it is common to find people on the fringes to have a more positive approach to life.

The energy of each Sun sign is transferred to the people born into it. Objects, people, and animals were used to illustrate the unique energy of each sign. This is why you hear people say they are a "ram" if they are the Sun sign, Aries. Below is a list of the different objects, people, or animals for each of the 12 Sun signs:

1. Aries- Ram
2. Taurus- Bull
3. Gemini- Twins
4. Cancer- Crab
5. Leo- Lion
6. Virgo- Virgin
7. Libra- Scales
8. Scorpio- Scorpion
9. Sagittarius- Centaur
10. Capricorn- Goat
11. Aquarius- Water carrier
12. Pisces- Fish

More on the Sun Signs
Aries: March 21- April 20
Pioneers and leaders. Leading and managing others makes those under this sign happy. They are inspirational and magnetic. Their dynamic approach to leadership is outgoing and motivational. They take risks, but only after carefully considering the outcomes, and are often prepared to courageously fight for causes they believe in. Busy-bodies, Arians like to work for themselves or as a leader in another enterprise. They are concerned about the affairs around them and are curious to understand how things "work." Sometimes, when working with a cautious or lingering person, they can get impatient. They want to know the heart of the issue quickly, and patience is hard for them at times. Social activities that allow them to talk and engage are the best social situations for Arians. As a friend, they are lively and warm.

Taurus: April 21- May 21
Determined, patient, and practical. Before jumping into action, those born under this sign are cautious and take time to think about the situation. Because of this slow-to-action trait, others may view them as obstinate or stubborn. It is true that those of this sign do like to do things in their own way and at their own time. Security is important to Taureans, so while they are generous, they do keep something back for themselves. Typically, good with money, their drive and determination serve their professional ambitions well. They like to be surrounded by beautiful things and look for balance and harmony in their environment. This means, when you walk into a Taurean home, there are tasteful and quality objects around you. When they make a purchase, it is of good quality. Taureans, however, can be very stubborn. Once they have made up their minds it is hard to change it. Sometimes it can almost seem impossible. This means they are unforgiving and inflexible at times. Controlling this trait will help keep them in harmony and peace, which is their normal demeanor.

Gemini: May 22- June 21
Thinking on their feet, Gemini's are restless and versatile. They are also ingenious! Social members of a community, those born under this sign are always thirsting for knowledge. They love to talk and share their knowledge through words to anyone who will listen. Any career where they can use their words and intellect is a good fit. Idle chatter though is a waste of time for Gemini's. They need

mental stimulation as well. Almost everyone gets along with a Gemini and it is in part due to their easy-going nature. They are typically artistic and creative, and very adaptable. Variety is necessary for their life, which can often lead to a lot of unfinished projects as they move on to something new and exciting. Projects that yield quick results in a short amount of time are typically best. The energy behind a Gemini is often nervous-feeling. They are often good mediators; however, because of their ability to see both sides of a situation.

Cancer: June 22- July 22

Imagination, emotion, and romance. Feelings are the governing force behind the actions and decisions of those under this sign. When pushed into a corner, cancers can fight back, but they will often find themselves hurt because of their high sensitivity. They are typically charming and captivating; which can be a great treat; however, it can be misused when a Cancerian uses this trait to manipulate and get what they want. They often enjoy the achievement of success because they tenaciously pursue their goals. While other signs are ruled by the Sun, this sign is actually ruled by the moon. This is why they tend to be more emotional and sensitive than other signs. This emotional sensitivity may lead to Cancerians being more guarded, for fear of being hurt. They may shy away from commitment in order to protect themselves. When they do take the risk and find a secure relationship, their home and family are strong. They are often excellent parents. Money is a challenge. While they love a bargain, they do tend to spend money frivolously and freely at times. Many Cancerians become excellent spiritual or psychic beings because of their intuition.

Leo: July 23- August 22

Friendly, open, determined, and ambitious. Natural leaders from birth and drawn to positions of power and leadership. They live life with enthusiasm and are often very honest and open in all areas of their life. People love to spend time with them because they are happy and positive, spreading this emotional state to others. No matter what they set their mind to they are determined and confident. You never miss a Leo. Unfortunately, their confidence can cause problems and delays, especially if they are overconfident in their abilities. Correcting this can be a challenge because of the pride of a Leo. Demeaning or perceived ridicule can be very negative. Flattery, on the other hand, can lead to unwanted behaviors as well, so there is a fine balance in the interactions with

Leo's. Big gestures and generosity are typical expressions of a Leo. No matter where they go or what they do they spread enthusiasm and warmth. They are good storytellers, and can often "embellish" the truth to deliver a good story.

Virgo: August 23 – September 23

Matter of fact, down to earth, and modest are the most common descriptions of a Virgo. They often look at life in a very shrewd manner. These people look tidy and respectable. They are conformists and naturally very cautious. They are also typically highly intelligent. Because of their attention to detail and precision in their actions they make great administrators or organizers. They also have a great memory. They often keep their thoughts to themselves; however, they do make judgments rather quickly. Their natural reservation can make it hard to connect to them, but when they are ready to let you in their inner circle, they are great friends. Perfectionism and high-standards for themselves can lead to a negative inner critic. They can obsess over the small details of a project and often fret about the completion of something because it often does not live up to their high expectations. They are internally motivated and like to work quietly behind the scenes. They do not need outlandish acknowledgment when a job is done well; they like to feel the inner satisfaction of it instead. When they perceive that something is unfair a Virgo can come across as critical and outspoken.

Libra: September 24 – October 22

Friendly, balanced, and harmonious. Sometimes indecisive. Confrontation and arguments are often avoided; however, talking is a great outlet and they enjoy sharing information with others. Sincerity and honesty are important for a Libra. They practice this in their daily life and expect others to do the same as well. They care deeply for the people in their lives, and their emotions "run deep." Their taste for good and beautiful things is typically very tasteful. The incision Librans can suffer from can lead to impatience in others, especially if they are indecisive about an unimportant decision. Once a decision is made; however, it is followed to the very end. They are very determined in their actions. They believe in playing fair and treating others fairly. They are often the champion of the underdog.

Scorpio: October 23 – November 21
Determined and forceful. Concentration is not an issue for those under this sign. It is hard to fully see a Scorpio, as they are often very guarded and reserved. They see and understand how people act, thanks to their strong intuition, but again they never really share too much of themselves to anyone else. They like to work and be alone more often than not and take calculated risks when necessary. They are very careful about their actions and decisions. They often wait for the "perfect" opportunity, and can sometimes use the element of "surprise" to their advantage. Scorpios often attain their goals because they are often very clear about what they want and are dogged in their pursuit to accomplish something.

Sagittarius: November 22- December 22
Optimistic, open, and friendly. Sagittarians have a zest for life and are enthusiastic. Loyal and honest but also tactless and outspoken at times. They need independence, so space and room are necessary for growth and development. Activities outdoors and sports are great areas for those born under this sign because of the independence and space necessary to thrive. Trying to do too much at one time is a problem, so learning how to channel energy is necessary. This is especially important in youth. Learning is important; however, it can feel restricted in a formal classroom. Independent learning is often preferred. Life, philosophy, vision, and foresight are all strengths of a Sagittarian.

Capricorn: December 23 – January 20
Hardworking, practical, and solid. Often serious and steady as they reach for their goals. Fair, careful, logical, and cautious. They achieve long-term, ambitious goals because they are careful planners. Capricorns like to work all the details out before taking action because of their conservative and practical nature. They are more careful and thriftier with money and like to save money rather than spend it. They often set a goal or choose a specific purpose for finances and work to achieve that. Emotional expression can be a challenge; however, when they find the right partner, they are very romantic. As a parent, they are very loving, responsible, and good. They love family life.

Aquarius: January 21- February 19
Lack of prejudice, unconventional, tolerant, broad-minded, sympathetic. Independent, altruistic, inventive, and intellectual. Love to help others and are often great humanitarians. Their ideas

are often radical and progressive and they tend to have a science-focused mind. Always looking forward, they like to turn their visions and dreams into real life. They are accepting of others and their unique traits. Their friendships are strong and long-lasting. They love the truth in their life and their actions. They use both their logic and their intuition. They are typically more on the mental plane than the spiritual.

Pisces: February 20 – March 20

Creative, philanthropic, thoughtful, imaginative, and gentle. Successful and popular in life, they can be indecisive and vague at times. Crises can occur when they are hurt emotionally or are disappointed because they are very sensitive. To get the best performance from them they need to have constant encouragement. Their sympathy for others is heightened by their intuition and receptivity. They are often great judges of a person's character but it often puts them in the path for hurt or disappointment. If they are dismissed or rebuffed when hurt they will often bottle their feelings up inside. They are the person others lean on when they are in need of support. They do best in a career that is designed to help others.

CHAPTER 7
Connections Between Tarot And Numerology

While some mystical arts are slightly linked to numerology, there is a direct connection between Tarot and Numerology. When you practice Tarot, applying your understanding of Numerology is important to get the most from your reading. Understanding Numerology can actually help you understand Tarot much faster and easier.

To begin, look at the minors, or the Aces to the tens. You can look at the meaning of the number compared to the meaning of the suit and see the overlaps. Below is a breakdown of the general characteristics of the suits:

Suit	*Meaning*
Cup	Peaceful, creative, intuitive, empathetic, emotions, relationships, love
Wand	Impulsive, creative, career-oriented, passionate, energetic, courageous, power, action, inspirational
Pentacle	Business-oriented, manifesting, education, prosperity, family-focused, fertile, home, and work, practical
Sword	Untruth and truth, writing, speaking, mental challenge or complexity, mental dexterity, communicative, ideation

The following chart now defines the numbers from Ace to ten:

Numbers	*Meaning*
Ace	Gift, beginnings, new ideation or project, potential, birth, insight

Two	Wait, choice, attraction, receptive, balanced, duality
Three	Expand, express, create, grow, fruitful, cooperation, increase
Four	Foundational, strength, organization, structured, secure, stable
Five	Change, loss, fluctuate, issues, unstable, challenging
Six	Adjustments, relaxed, increasing stability, recovering, healing, comforting, peaceful, harmonious
Seven	Individual, independent, faithful, knowing, discovering, spiritual, questioning, assessment
Eight	Fortitude, courageous, accomplishment, self-motivated, progressive, movement or lack of movement
Nine	Knowledge, insight, self-understanding, awakening, achievement, getting near the end
Ten	Finality, beginnings or the space between the end and the beginning of something new.

Understanding the combination of the two concepts together you gain a better idea of the minor arcana. Knowing this, apply the information to the reading and you or your seeker's issue at hand.

While Numerology can be easy to learn once you know the meaning behind the 11 numbers in the science, Tarot can be more challenging and intimidating, especially if you are beginning your exploration of Tarot. Thankfully, there are patterns and repetitions in the cards that can be helpful in learning the mysteries revealed in your deck. Each deck has numbers listed on the various cards. This is where your background in Numerology comes in handy.

In your Tarot deck, there are 78 different cards. Of those cards, there are two categories; the Major and the Minor Arcana. Even if you are not very familiar with a card in the deck if you know the correspondence and difference of the Major or Minor Arcana and the number on the card you can improve your grasp of the card. There are 22 cards reserved for the Major Arcana. These show the major events or occurrences in someone's path of life. They are archetypes and are "big picture." The numbers on these cards start at zero and go to 21. The passage from innocence and childhood through to enlightenment and maturity are expressed through the symbolic characters of the Major Arcana cards. The rest of the deck is Minor Arcana. They relate to the physical world and are separated into four suits, as outlined above. Like a common deck of playing cards, there are numbers from Ace to ten, but this deck also includes the Page as a "court" card. Each suite also has a related element to it.

The numbers on the cards all reveal an underlying pattern or theme among them. For example, The Ace of Pentacles, Cups, Swords, and Wands, as well as the Magician card all, have the Number 1 on it. While their exact meanings are all different, they all have the same thread of new beginnings running through them. There is a cycle to Numerology and Tarot, which is also a compatible relationship between the two. Odd numbers illustrate change and instability. Even numbers are enduring and stable. In addition, as a Tarot card signifies an end, it also signifies a beginning, because all things move from "birth" to "death" and on and on.

To help you further understand this relationship, below is a brief introduction to Tarot. This introduction is meant to offer a basic understanding of Tarot to help you see the relationship it has to Numerology. If you want to learn more about Tarot, it is advisable to look for additional reading on the subject.

An Introduction to Tarot

If you try to explain to a typical person off the street that you are going to study Tarot, they may question you and wonder how it is possible to tell the mysteries of the Universe with a deck of cards.

This is a common view and doubt many have about this science. But when you see how the cards work and reveal solutions to your problems in life, you will begin to understand the difference Tarot can make.

Like many ancient arts and sciences, the origin of it is uncertain. There is a record from Italy where Tarot-like cards were used as a sort of game. There are still beautiful versions of these early Tarot cards still in existence. Wealthy patrons commissioned artistic cards for this game and are quite beautiful. One of the most complete and earliest decks still in existence is the Visconti-Sforza, which was designed in about 1450. A group of occult scholars in the 19th and 18th centuries began using the cards. While at first, they began using the cards as a game, the group quickly realized that they were more powerful than just a mere parlor game. This group was the one responsible for connecting the cards to various mystical systems like alchemy, Kabbalah, hermetic philosophy, and mysteries from Egypt. They revealed or developed the connections and the known history of Tarot. Once this occult group discovered the great potential of the cards, they worked for centuries to uncover more. And during this time, more societies, especially secret ones, incorporated Tarot into their practices. One of the more popular groups is the Order of the Golden Dawn.

Now, as new perspectives shift, Tarot has moved from traditional occults to more mainstream. Decks reflecting these new interests now exist, including Japanese, dragon, herbal, and Native American decks. With this expansion, Tarot has risen to be the most popular method for divination. In atypical reading, there is a seeker, or someone searching for an answer to a personal issue or question, and a reader, or someone who knows how to read the cards. The seeker must shuffle and cut a deck of cards. The reader then divides and arranges the cards that the seeker chose in a spread or a certain pattern. The meaning of each position in the spread is defined, just as each card has a meaning. It is the combination of the position in the spread and the card meaning that the reader interprets. This is what offers advice to the seeker and their problem or question.

The reality of the reading is that it is a simple process; however, it is often not presented or observed in a simple manner. Most of the time you see a portrayal of Tarot as a speedy process in a back room, shadowed and evil. It is typically a mystical-looking old woman that looks mysterious and shady, reading a series of cards to young and anxious young lay. The old woman creepily lifts a card and lays it slowly in front of the girl, revealing the Death Card. The girl becomes afraid and sees oncoming death and doom in her near future. This is the most common Hollywood interpretation of Tarot. It is still very common to attach darkness and negativity to Tarot. Many religions rebuke Tarot and view it as an unreasonable system of understanding. For a better understanding, try to put aside these perceptions and presentations, and look at the information of the Tarot instead. You can even just begin at the very basic; that a deck of Tarot cards is a collection of pictures. Now, what can you do with those pictures?

This is not a question for your logical, conscious mind. The answer sits in your deeper awareness and memory. And the answer is not found in your typical or everyday life. It is normal to ignore your unconscious, but it is something that affects your daily actions constantly. Sigmund Freud valued and stressed the unconscious' aspects of primitiveness and irrationality. Carl Jung also emphasized the unconscious, particularly the creative and positive sides of it. He illustrated how the unconscious engages in the various qualities of the entire Universe. It is possible that we will never really uncover the true potential and power of the unconscious mind. There are things we will probably never unravel. Despite this, there are things that you can do to help peel off some of the layers of mystery. There are several techniques to do this, such as meditation, visualization, dream readings, and psychotherapy for example. Tarot is also a method to do this.

To help you realize how reading occurs, consider the suit of Swords and the number five. There is an image of a man in the foreground holding three swords. There are two swords at his feet. In the middle ground are two men. A person may look at this image and see a man who has won a battle and is happy, while the other two are downcast at their loss. This means the person with this interpretation looked at an image and created their own interpretation or projection of a story onto the card. It may seem like the only and obvious interpretation; however, someone else may see something completely different. It is possible someone sees a man trying to help the other two, or trying to break up a feud between the other two. The image is really open-ended. There are many possibilities. The reason one person sees something and another sees something different is because it is human nature to project your unconscious on objects in your environment. You also see your reality through the tinted lenses of your own internal state of being. There are other common therapeutic methods for supporting this process, such as the Rorschach inkblot test.

This is one of the major reasons the Tarot cards are some valuable. Projection is a powerful revelation and tool. The patterns and images are great at tapping into your unconscious. This is also the very personal and individual part of a Tarot deck. There is also a collective aspect of the Tarot deck. There are common experiences and needs that we need as humans. The images on the cards capture these common moments. Using this familiarity, the images draw out the reactions to such encounters. It is common to have people react to a card in a similar way because of the archetype represented on the card. Using the observation of human perception and subconscious, Tarot cards have changed over thousands of years to illustrate an assembly of foundational patterns of emotions and thoughts.

To help illustrate this concept more fully, bring to mind or find an image of the Empress card in a Tarot deck. On this card, she symbolizes the idea of the Mother and the principle of the Mother. She represents the abundance in life. The image is designed to bring to show luxury. The pillows she sits on are lush and soft in appearance. The robe she wears flows around her in rich folds and drapes. There is a feeling of sensual and bountiful abundance of Nature itself. This commonality in reaction to this card is a powerful example of how some cards are designed to be more universal than personal.

It is the combination of the universal and the individual. It is the support of the commonality that provides a space for individual expression. You see a card in your own way, but some in the same way as thousands of others. Your own awareness is reflected back at you, like a mirror, when you are the seeker in a Tarot reading.

The actions in dealing the cards are important. The seeker is instructed to shuffle and cut the deck, while the reader is the one that deals the cards. And while the cards may feel random, there is still a subconscious intervention at play, making the cards that are chosen special. There are certain cards that you need and are meant to interact with to help guide you to understanding. That is the point of Tarot reading. To further examine the point of "random," think about what that means. "Random" often refers to the feeling of chance or an event that occurs because of some sort of un-meddled force. This means, that in a situation like this, there is a variety of outcomes possible, but only one occurs, and there is no real reason why this happened. There are two critical assumptions in the term "random," There is no reason or purpose to why an outcome occurred, and there are forces at work making things happen.

Knowing how you view a "chance" or "random" result helps you better understand why some things appear random but are really not. To begin, the act of Tarot readings is not an un-meddled force. There are very conscious and intentional actions taking place. As a reader, you chose to study Tarot and learn how to use the cards. You may even buy your own special deck of cards. Even the way you shuffle and cut the deck is intentional and personal to you. And finally, the way you read the cards is intentional and non-mechanical. Each step of the process is highly involved. This means that a Tarot reading is certainly not an un-meddled force. It is easier to claim it is random because to explain how you're conscious and subconscious worked to deliver the results is not possible. Your conscious did not deliberately choose the cards, so it is easier to say it is "chance" rather than diving into the idea of the powerful subconscious "meddling" in your reality. It is possible for your inner, subconscious to engage in your outer, real life in ways you cannot completely comprehend. It is a hard truth to acknowledge, but something profound to ponder.

The other part of the definition of "random" is the idea that the result came about for no particular purpose. The assumption is that there is not meant for the result. It is possible to not always recognize the meaning behind the purpose of a result, but does that mean there is no purpose? Is it irrelevant if the purpose is small, or more critical if the purpose is larger in the grand scheme of things in your life? What if you have many little results that stack up to create a large result? Is that different? How can you tell, especially at the moment? Can you assume that if you cannot tell if a result has a purpose that it is not significant in your growth? For example, if you roll a die, and get a four, and the next time you roll it you get a six, is the meaning of the number you roll the same? Are the results equal?

Many religions say that "everything happens for a reason." This does not apply to just the big things, but to the little things as well. Sometimes, the things you do years ago can be a lesson at the moment but also a tool for sharing and teaching later in life. Meaning is a real mystery. This occurs when your outer reality intermingles with your inner landscape. You use your inner wisdom to decipher the message you are receiving from your outer experience. But you can only decipher the message when you are open and receptive to it. Tarot offers several messages through the connections and images on the cards. In addition, a Tarot reading also shares the meaning in them because of the perceptions you bring to them. You transfer your desires and truths to what you read. When you are open to exposing your most inner and deepest truths, you have a chance to reveal more of yourself.

The meaning you get from reading is really a reflection of your internal Self that is connected with the divine. It can be called your subconscious or unconscious, but those that practice Tarot understand that it is much more than that. It is like you have a wise guide living inside; a person that knows you better than you know yourself. This can be called the Soul in some circles. It is this guide or higher self that shares the meaning with you. Because they are with you since conception, your higher self or guide is always with you and knows you before you had thoughts and memories. It is not possible to kill or remove this, but it is possible to silence or ignore it.

Your guide becomes alert when you gather your Tarot cards and start reading. You are telling your higher self that you are ready for meaning and purpose. It is a faithful act and you have to trust in the guidance from inside. It is always there; this is just a way to tap into it. As humans, we are designed to trust in our intuition or internal guide, yet for some reason, we have forgotten how to awaken and listen to it. Instead of looking deep inside for the answer we seek to understand in our conscious mind. While your conscious mind is clever, it is simply not aware enough to make the best decisions for your overall path in life. It seems a piece of the picture, but your higher self sees so much more than the big picture. If you find yourself feeling like things are happening to you and it is random or by chance, you are not connected to your higher self. You are connected to your conscious mind. This leads to great suffering because you can end up feeling purposeless and listless. As you access your internal guide, you become clear on exactly who you are and what your purpose is. Life is different; filled with peace and certainty.

CHAPTER 8
Relationship Compatibility

In your life, romantic relationships are a unique connection, and it helps to have a better understanding of how you will mesh with a potential partner, or even understand why your partner is behaving or choosing the things they are. Thankfully, with Numerology, you can receive some guidance with romantic relationships. Your Life Path number is important to know, as well as the Life Path number of your romantic connection. Keep in mind that there are six numbers for each of you, plus additional sequences of numbers which you will learn about later in this book, that combine together to make you a unique person. The same goes for your partner. This means comparing your Compatibility on just your Life Path numbers is not the most accurate method. It is a start. If you want to dive in further, look at your numbers combined to find out what will mesh and what will resist in the relationship.

For now, to help you get started in determining compatibility, identify your Life Path number below and learn a bit more about what other Life Path number generally fit with you and which do not. There is also a brief breakdown of each number in a list at the end of the Life Path compatibility explanation for a quick reference. To help you determine your Life Path number, refer back to the earlier chapters in this book to calculate it. Once you have your number, look for it in the following sections to read about your potential matches!

Life Path Number 1

A Life Path number 1 meshes well with those with a Life Path number 5 or 3. This is because these two numbers are easy-going enough to handle an opinionated and sometimes bossy number 1. 3 especially is optimistic and easygoing. This goes well with the self-conscious and serious personality of a number 1, mainly because a number 3 ignores and lightens this behavior. As a number 1, you like to be in charge. A number 1 will make this lighter, while a number 5 will bring energy and adventure to this serious side. Of course, a number 6 finds harmony in this relationship as well, but this is really because a number 6 gets along with just about anyone.

Connecting with another 1 can be passionate and intense, but it is often short-lived. When two 1's get together it is like having too many cooks in the kitchen. Two captains are trying to steer the ship. This can make the relationship strained and challenging. Another relationship that causes strain is number 8. They are entrepreneurial and authoritative, and this is like having another 1 in the relationship; can be passionate but often short-lived. These two numbers find themselves competing for more than connecting. A number 2 is sometimes a good partner; however, these connections tend to be better in work or personal life and not romantically. A number 2 is sensitive and gentle, with a diplomatic outlook. The combination is good, but not passionate. Similarly, a number 7 is a good connection, but not romantically. A number 7 provides introspection and spirituality to a number 1, and often is a great guide or tutor to you, but romantically two numbers are not the best fit. Instead, look to a number 7 as a trusted friend to help you grow to higher levels of intuition and enlightenment.

If You Are A Life Path Number 1, And Your Partner Is …. The Compatibility Is ….

The following list outlines your compatibility with each number as a quick reference guide.

Your Partner's Life Path Number	You Compatibility with Them
1	Good at times, bad at times
2	Compatible, but can be boring
3	Compatible, but needy
4	Uptight and challenging
5	Natural connection but independence is necessary
6	Struggle for power at times
7	A wise connection but can be boring
8	Very volatile, think of oil and water
9	Deep love and connection but can be too intense

Life Path Number 2

A Life Path Number 2 meshes well with a number 8, or a visionary, and the number 9, or the humanitarian. A Life Path number 2 is often more subtle and compliments the business-focused, industrious, and decisive traits of a Life Path number 8. In fact, a number 8 and a number 2 is great both romantically and professionally. A Life Path Number 9 relates well with a Life Path Number 2 because they are typically composed and classy, but also a little aloof. Life Path Number 6 is a good match because they are loving, forgiving, and protective.

It may at first seem like a Life Path Number 4 is a good fit with a Number 2, because they are dependable and down-to-earth; however, they may end up being too boring for you. This is the same with a Life Path Number 7. They are introverted and serious, which can be too boring for a Number 2. You could potentially match well with a Life Path Number 1, but it is essential to the roles of each partner are well defined. For example, a number 1 always wants the last word, but as a 2, you can manipulate the situation to determine what that word will be. As a Life Path number 2, this manipulation or influence is a natural trait you possess. A relationship that is sure not to be boring is with a Life Path Number 5. They bring adventure, passion, and wonder to the relationship. Be careful with this combination; however. As number 5 is often over-indulgent and irresponsible, bringing tumult to the feminine and vulnerable 2. This is somewhat similar to the Life Path Number 3. The relationship may be full of passion, but the lack of focus and discipline in a Number 3 ends up leaving you as a number 2 holding on to all the responsibility. This means you carry more than your fair share, and that can be hazardous.

If You Are A Life Path Number 2, And Your Partner Is ....
The Compatibility Is ....
The following list outlines your compatibility with each number as a quick reference guide.

Your Partner's Life Path Number	*You Compatibility with Them*
1	Good at times, bad at times
2	Love that is sensitive
3	Lots of laughing and love
4	A marriage-worthy match

5	Sometimes opposites do attract
6	The family commitment is strong here
7	You may find your true Self being challenged
8	The first thing that is a priority is family
9	Each looks to save one another

Life Path Number 3

A Life Path Number 3 enjoys wonderful relationships with number 7 and number 5. A Life Path Number 5, in particular, is great because of the adventure and daring it brings to the relations, 5's are also known for their adaptability, which meshes well with a Life Path Number 3. A Number 3 often craves chaps and unpredictability, and a Number 5 delivers. On the other hand, a number 7 offers a little mysticism and introversion to the relationship, which is quieter but still compatible. This combination creates a deep relationship and an appreciation for experiences in life. In all of Numerology and relationships, the combination of a 3 and 7 is particularly significant. When these two come together, romantically or otherwise, they tend to lift each other higher and encourage one another to be bigger than the individual alone.

While it may seem good to have a sense of grounding in your life as a Life Path Number 3, a romantic Life Path Number 4 partner is not what it appears. Often the two spirals off of one another in a negative manner, bringing out the worst. In addition, a partner with a Life Path Number 8 may seem like a good fit because of their physicality and authoritative nature, you will find this criticism and unrelenting nature tiresome. Even though a number 1 may be critical, the combination of a 1 and 3 tend to work better in relationships. This connection is often a very nice combination. To support a long-lasting and fruitful relationship, consider a Life Path Number 2. These people bring intuition and forgiveness to your relationships, and there is often a beautiful balance struck here. Interestingly, a person with a Life Path Number 6, which is notorious for getting along with just about everyone, does not tend to get along well with a number 3. And a Number 3 does not usually like the connection with a number 6! This is mostly because number 3 is undisciplined and flighty. It can drive a Number 6 cray. In addition, connecting with another number 3 is a recipe for disaster. Two number 3's are too unfocused and undisciplined for success.

If You Are A Life Path Number 3, And Your Partner Is ....
The Compatibility Is ....
The following list outlines your compatibility with each number as a quick reference guide.

Your Partner's Life Path Number	You Compatibility with Them
1	Good at times, bad at times
2	Love that is sensitive
3	Naturally connected
4	Passionate but planned and structured
5	A lot of fun and socializing
6	Creative together
7	Opposite personalities but can be a passionate affair
8	A lot of work and a fight for independence often
9	Communication and love come naturally

Life Path Number 4

No other number craves a long-lasting and firm relationship than you, Life Path Number 4. It is not because of your fear of being alone, but rather because you love the lifestyle of routine and solidify a relationship like this offers. Because of this desire for stability and grounding, you will want to steer clear of the restless and dynamic Life Path Number 5 and the unpredictable and playful Life Path Number 3. Instead, look to 8 and 1 to offer determination, focus, and goal-orientation in your life. A Life Path Number 8 is a great match because the discipline and organization of an 8 and a 4 complement each other well, and a number 8 also bring a vision to the relationship. You bring the focus on details as a number 4, while they bring the "big picture," and together the two of you can be unstoppable. This is true in romance as well as business.

Another good match is the Life Path Number 6. They are nurturing and caring. Be cautious, when these two get together it typically results in a lot of children. A Life Path Number 9 is a dreamer and idealistic. This does not mesh well with our practical and grounded nature. But, the introspective, spiritual, and wondering Life Path Number 7 brings a balance and dynamic admiration to the Life Path Number 4. This is a beautiful relationship when it blossoms.

If You Are A Life Path Number 4, And Your Partner Is .... The Compatibility Is ....

The following list outlines your compatibility with each number as a quick reference guide.

Your Partner's Life Path Number	You Compatibility with Them
1	Good at times, bad at times
2	Love that is sensitive
3	Naturally connected
4	Good for a long-term relationship
5	Miscommunication is a major problem
6	Good home life and feels very secure
7	Wonderful, stable, and secure
8	Goals and dreams may align but can be testy
9	Your world view may be challenged, and that can be hard to get over

Life Path Number 5

A Life Path Number 5 enjoys the possibility of a great number or romantic partners. The problem does not lie incompatibility or creation but in the longevity. This lies with your partner of choice, not with your Life Path Number 5. Yes, you are a devoted and loyal partner, but you need constant change and are often restless. This means your partner cannot demand too much from you, but also cannot be too predictable. A Life Path Number 1 is an obvious choice, thanks to their courageous and daring nature, but so does Life Path Number 3, who is often optimistic, imaginative, and playful. A Life Path Number 6 is a nurturing and caring match, also because they are sacrificing and protective, which a number 5 needs often. What may be surprising is that Life Path Number 7 is a good match. They are earnest and spiritual, providing a constant challenge to the number 5. There is a beautiful harmony struck with this pairing. A number 5 is often impatient, dynamic, and self-indulgent, while the number 7 is reclusive and solemn. When these two combine they bring out the best in each other.

It may look like at first a number 4 and number 5 would be a good match, but sometimes this combination ends up in devastation. The number 4 can be offended by your undisciplined and changing nature while you get bored with their predictable, practical, and stable tendencies. And while it is possible for a number 9 and number 8 to develop strong connections with a number 5, they will most likely not be willing to tolerate your desire for something new all the time. They are too goal-oriented or responsible for this constant upheaval of life.

A general principle for companionship and numerology is to not pair similar Life Path Numbers with one another; however, two Life Path Number 5's can be a match made in heaven. All the other numbers may not make great romantic relationships, but 5's are the exception. When two 5's come together their partnership is passionate, adventurous, and never boring. Their natural tendency is for adventure and freedom, so an outdoor lifestyle is great for that need for freedom. The trick to this relationship is moderation. 5's tend to be overindulgent and can go to extremes with things like sex, alcohol, eating, etc. If the two 5's are not in check, this can lead to horrible consequences.

If You Are A Life Path Number 5, And Your Partner Is ....
The Compatibility Is ....
The following list outlines your compatibility with each number as a quick reference guide.

Your Partner's Life Path Number	You Compatibility with Them
1	Good at times, bad at times
2	Love that is sensitive
3	Naturally connected
4	Good for a long-term relationship

5	Passionate, intense and free
6	The opposite end of the spectrum, and attract nicely
7	Drama, drama, drama, but can be deep
8	Troublesome yet dynamic
9	A powerful couple for the short-term, but often peters out

Life Path Number 6

A Life Path Number 6 gets along with just about any other number, short term or long term. You have a sacrificing nature and are willing to be the safety net for others. This makes you a safe and secure partner. You are also unbound with your love and caring for others, which can make you humanity's favorite partner. That being said, it is like you have the ability to choose who and what you want to be challenged with. Some partnerships are more suitable to your nature than others. For example, the Life Path Number 2 is gentle and sensitive. You and they are guided by the heart, not the mind, and harmonize well together. A Life Path Number 9 is also a great partner because of their sympathetic and conscientious approach to relationships. A number 8, for their strength, and a number 1, for their drive, are also good matches. A troublesome match could be a self-indulgent number 5 or the unfocused number 3. In fact, a Life Path Number 3 may be the one pairing you might want to avoid.

If You Are A Life Path Number 6, And Your Partner Is ....
The Compatibility Is ....

The following list outlines your compatibility with each number as a quick reference guide.

Your Partner's Life Path Number	You Compatibility with Them
1	Good at times, bad at times
2	Love that is sensitive
3	Naturally connected
4	Good for a long-term relationship
5	Passionate, intense and free

6	These two are the cutest things you have ever seen!
7	It may take an effort to make this one work
8	So much affection, especially publicly...
9	The connection is intuitive and intense

Life Path Number 7

A Life Path Number 7 tends to have trouble with marriage. If you do get married, it is unlikely that it will last longer. This is not because you have a problem with relationships, or that you cannot form meaningful relationships, but rather because your expectations and dreams are too hard for anyone to live up to. You are critical and judgmental, which can cause you to leave relationships behind as you search for what could live up to your standards. This is not always a bad thing! You are independent and do not rely on a romantic relationship to enjoy your life. This is unlike many other numbers. Marriage typically occurs later in life, but not because they want children or a family. A marriage typically occurs because a number 7 found someone who challenges their intellect and has insight enough to allow space and quiet to allow a number 7 to dream and contemplate. Two of the most challenging, but in a good way, numbers for a romantic relationship are the intellectually-developed number 5 and the creative and witty number 3. The spontaneity of a number 5 is attractive to you, and the imagination of a number 3 helps you push your dreams past your own limitations.

Connecting with a number 2 is not your favorite. They are sentimental and superficial, which can be unacceptable to you. A number 1 is too controlling. A number 8 is often too connected to material items, which is against your internal value system of spiritual over the material. Finally, a number 9 is typically too aloof for you. You are more introverted, like number 9, but you are not distant from relationships. The great part of a relationship with a number 7 is that once you make that connection, you are deep and open. You do not keep separate or secrets from your partner.

***If You Are A Life Path Number 7, And Your Partner Is ....
The Compatibility Is ....***

The following list outlines your compatibility with each number as a quick reference guide.

Your Partner's Life Path Number	You Compatibility with Them
1	Good at times, bad at times
2	Love that is sensitive
3	Naturally connected
4	Good for a long-term relationship
5	Passionate, intense and free
6	These two are the cutest things you have ever seen!
7	Strong connection mentally, but maybe not physically
8	A strong physical connection
9	Toxic

Life Path Number 8

A Life Path Number 8 likes control. This means, in a romantic relationship, you look for a partner you can guide and control a bit. It is not about having a doormat of a partner, but someone who can compromise for you. You are domineering and do not like to compromise. This is why a 6 and a 2 are good matches for you. A number 6 is loving and sacrificing, while the number 2 is nurturing and caring. Be wary of a number 1. They also like to be in control and can have trouble letting you take the lead. Most likely they will look to fight you at every turn because they do not like your vying for control. Number 5 is also not a good fit because they love their freedom and change, which is not something you embrace. Also, the number 3, while creative and adaptable, is also irresponsible and too flaky for you. You limit your potential romantic partners because you are unwilling to let someone else "wear the pants" in your connections.

A Life Path Number 8 has a unique ability to find balance in the material and spiritual realms; however, the number 7 does not see past the materiality of your nature. This is why many 7's will not give you a chance, despite the potential for a good pairing. If a 7 can get past your material side and challenge you on a spiritual plane, you can have a good relationship here. Number 4 is one of your best matches. They are not easily controlled by you because they control themselves, but you enjoy the similarities in your nature. You are both stable, grounded, logical, practical, disciplined, focused on your goals, and methodical. This relationship works romantically, but it is perhaps even better when working together because each one supplements the other. You see the big picture, and the number 4 gets down to the details.

If You Are A Life Path Number 8, And Your Partner Is ....
The Compatibility Is ....
The following list outlines your compatibility with each number as a quick reference guide.

Your Partner's Life Path Number	*You Compatibility with Them*
1	Good at times, bad at times
2	Love that is sensitive
3	Naturally connected
4	Good for a long-term relationship
5	Passionate, intense and free
6	These two are the cutest things you have ever seen!
7	Strong connection mentally, but maybe not physically
8	Too controlling, each seeking respect
9	Different approaches to life are too diverse

Life Path Number 9

A Life Path Number 9 is possibly the most challenged in terms of romantic relationships. You like to be distant and secret. You do not like to expose your true self to anyone. You hate feeling vulnerable. In addition, you feel that revealing yourself is unsophisticated and lacks class. This is a little aristocratic and can be harmful You do have the ability to be a loyal and good friend, but even to people close to you, you do not share your deepest desires or fears. This means, when you begin a relationship, you go very slowly and ready to run at a moment's notice.

Some Life Path numbers can see through this shield you put up, like a Life Path Number 2, who is intuitive and sensitive to others. They are a good match with you. A Life Path Number 6 is another good match because you have a lot in common with them. You both have a tendency to want to help others, are a bit idealistic, value community, and are genuine in your interactions with others. Another good connection for you is a Life Path Number 3. You both are imaginative, artistic, and creative. A number 3 brings humor to the relationship, which can help balance your more intense outlook.

You would do best to avoid a relationship with a Life Path Number 5 and the quirky number 7. In addition, a number 1, which is the total opposite of you, number 9, can see alluring for romance, but you two do not mesh well together. It is possible to have a romantic relationship with a 1, because of the opposite sides of the spectrum balance each other out, but in a working relationship, you can find it challenging and cumbersome.

If You Are A Life Path Number 9, And Your Partner Is ....
The Compatibility Is ....
The following list outlines your compatibility with each number as a quick reference guide.

Your Partner's Life Path Number	*You Compatibility with Them*
1	Good at times, bad at times
2	Love that is sensitive
3	Naturally connected
4	Good for a long-term relationship
5	Passionate, intense and free
6	These two are the cutest things you have ever seen!
7	Strong connection mentally, but maybe not physically
8	Too controlling, each seeking respect
9	It is like two old souls coming together, not much of a spark but can burn for a long time

CHAPTER 9
Cycle Of Change

As you learn more about your life through your primary six numbers, you can later apply this understanding of numerology to other areas of your life, including the periods of change or transition. Change throughout your life is constant. Sometimes you know when these changes will occur, while other times you seem to wake up one day and realize that everything is different now. Thankfully, you can use numerology to help reveal when these changes will take place and the meaning behind such changes. Your birthdate is what is used to calculate the various times of change in your life. There are two primary calculations used. The first is called the "cycle period," which is your birth date revealing what time things will change, and the second is the "cycle number," which use the birthdate and sometimes your name to determine the meaning of the change. Throughout this chapter, you will learn a bit more about various types of changes that will occur in your lifetime and some basic information about each cycle. Links to more information about each one is also included if you want to investigate further.

In general, your periods of change or cycles of change take place on your birthday. This is typically occurring on your date of birth, but it can change based on the calendar. For example, your personal year changes over when the new year begins, not on your date of birth. To help clarify when changes will occur, each following section will have this information outlined for you. Also, changes do not occur instantaneously. Most changes evolve over a period of time. There is typically not a sharp change of energy from one day to the next, so be prepared for the gradual adjustment as your mind and body prepare for the new cycle.

The Power Cycle

This is a single cycle change. It is considered a change from being ineffective to be effective. You use both your name and your birthdate to calculate this information. Once you find your number, it will not change. In all of numerology, this change is the longest cycle. While your number never changes, the energy behind the number can. The vibration of the number becomes more effective with the change in the cycle. Also, this calculation does not reveal an exact date to expect this change. It does not necessarily occur on your date of birth or at the start or end of a new year. It varies from person to person. In general, this change happens in the middle of a person's life, usually around the age of 40. This change brings about different priorities and values over time. It is a gradual change, but people may feel it happened suddenly when they finally notice all the shifts in focus.

This is when your outlook on life dramatically shifts. Sometimes the change is wildly drastic and other times for people it is more subtle. The power of change lies in the change of number and its relationship to your core number. If your power number is unique from your core number, the change is more resonant. If your power number is the same as your core number, the current outlook on life is enhanced but not altered. This means the change is less obvious.

Below is a brief chart to help you understand the meaning behind your power number:

1. Original, independent, ambitious, comfortable being alone, self-sufficient, good leader, inventor, or creator, ideas person.
2. Builds and sustains relationships, brings people together, diplomatic, team player, good peacemaker.
3. A full life, social, self-expressive, inspiring, optimistic, tolerant, good artist and motivator.
4. Bring loose ends together, accomplishes outstanding tasks, stable, strengthens the foundation, good worker who is reliable and pragmatic.
5. Active, variety, enjoys the experience, good with knowledge and sharing many talents.
6. Homebody, harmonious, nurturing, healer, good protector, healer, or teacher, homemaker.
7. Intuitive, personally focused, introspective, student, seeks understanding and wisdom, good philosopher or spiritualist.
8. Enjoys material possessions, organized, achiever, recognized for great accomplishments, authority figure, good financial person, politician, or executive, builder of societal value.
9. Compassionate, tolerant, broadminded, facilitator, humanitarian, good philanthropist or making a difference in their community or the world at large.

The Life Period Cycle

While the Power Cycle only has one change, the Life Period has three different cycles. Your birthdate is used to calculate both the cycle period and the cycle number. As described earlier in this book, the life period's first cycle begins at birth and runs until somewhere between your 27th and 35th year. The second cycle lasts for nine years. The final cycle picks up after the second cycles ninth year and runs to the end of your life. These changes occur on your birth date. Sometimes the transition takes several months to a year or more to occur.

The Pinnacle Years

It can sometimes be confused for your Life Period cycle, but there are four Pinnacle cycle years in your life. Like your Life Period cycles, you use your birth date to determine both the cycle's numbers and periods. The first cycle happens from birth to between your 27th and 35th year. The next two cycles occur for nine years respectively. The final cycle, your fourth Pinnacle Year Cycle, happens after the end of the third cycle, and it goes until your death. Your Pinnacle year cycles change over on your date of birth. It can take months for these changes to occur, but it is a shorter transition period than a Life Period Cycle most of the time.

The Challenges

There is some debate about how to calculate your challenges by Pythagorean Numerologist practitioners. No matter what method is used, your birth date is the source for determining your cycle periods and cycle numbers. One method aligns with your Life Period cycles while the other method aligns with the Pinnacle Year cycles. Like both of those periods of change, the Challenges transition on your birth date. There is a period of transition for each Challenge change. This transition can take months or more than a year.

One method for calculating your challenge numbers is to work with your birth date and reduce it to a single digit. In calculating challenge numbers, you will reduce Master Numbers to single digits as well. Also, keep in mind that there is no Challenge Number 9. There are four numbers for your Challenge Cycle. Each is a challenge you will struggle with at different parts of your life, as well as a "primary" challenge that lasts your entire life span. To begin one calculation to find these numbers, reduce your birth date to single digits for the month, day and year. For example, someone born on January 8th, 1985 would have the 1 for the month (January = 1), 8 for the day, and 5 for the year (1 + 9 + 8 + 5 = 23 = 2 + 3 = 5). The challenge numbers to start are 1, 8 and 5.

Now, to find the first Challenge Number, start by subtracting the month from the day. In this example, it would be 8 − 1= 7. The first Challenge Number is 7. To find your second Challenge Number, subtract the day number from the year number. In this example, it would be 5 − 8 = -3 or 3. In the event the result is negative, simply remove the negative sign in the beginning to reveal a positive number. There are no negative numbers in numerology. The third number you calculate is the third Challenge Number and is also your primary challenge. Find this by subtracting your answer from the first Challenge from the answer from the second Challenge. The example is 3 − 7 = -4 or 4. The final challenge is the month number subtracted from the year number. For example, 1 − 8 = -7 or 7.

Below is a chart to help you decipher the meaning of your challenges:

1. This number can occur. When it does it signifies that no challenge or certain area is more challenging than another. It means you face a myriad of different challenges which can all lead to great strength later in life. If you have this number, focus on developing and having confidence in your abilities. You are working on becoming a well-rounded person.
2. Learn to speak your truth and be independent. If this is one of your challenges, you may find yourself seeking approval from others often. You base your self-worth on the opinions of others. Find your value in what makes you unique.
3. Learn to balance your emotions. Do not let criticism dampen your spirits. You struggle asserting yourself and often avoid responsibility for fear of ownership. Do not let yourself shrink from taking on tasks, you can handle it and it is ok for people to depend on your skills.
4. Learn to complete the tasks you begin. Multi-tasking is fine, but as long as it does not get in the way of your goals. Take a moment before you react to a situation. Find a way to express yourself and your feelings that is productive and healthy.

5. Learn how to work hard to accomplish your goals. Do not procrastinate, like you want to. It is good to test your limits every now and then instead of following the well-worn path you enjoy. Discover how you can be more efficient and assertive in your work.
6. Learn how to control your impulses. Curb your reckless behavior. Typically, this number represents freedom and adventure but as a challenge, it indicates these areas of your life are extreme. Work on self-discipline and foresight.
7. Learn how to be more accepting. You tend to strive for perfection in yourself and others. This makes you cynical, authoritative, and critical. Find a way to lighten up and find unconditional love for yourself and others.
8. Learn how to be more open-minded to the logic of others. You tend to be overly-analytical and often dismiss concepts that you do not think are the "norm." You also struggle with expressing your emotions. Take time to enjoy new experiences and try new things to expand your world-view.
9. Learn how to let go of material objects. Money and social status are too important for a person with Challenge Number 8. You base your self-worth and value on these external objects. This can lead to unethical business choices to gain these material desires. Find a way to balance your spiritual needs with your material ones.
10. There is no Number 9 for challenges.

The Essence Transit

This change happens every year. It goes from one birthday to the next. The numbers on each birth date are calculated from your name. It is likely that the number will be the same year after year, for many years in a row. When there is a change, you can experience start its transition a few months prior to your birth date to a few weeks after. The numbers are calculated year after year using a letter from each segment of your name, including your first, middle and last name, if applicable. If you have more than one middle name you will have an additional number to add to the equation. If you do not have a middle name, you will only have your first and last name to calculate.

Below is an interpretation of the numbers for your Essence Transit numbers:

1. Begin improvements, discover new, the energy of new. Independent action. Decisive, active, leader, self-determined.
2. Partnerships, intuition, understanding. Peaceful, diplomatic, cooperative, team player.
3. Creativity and self-expression. Expressions through culture-related fields like decorating, literature, art, or music. Tolerant, optimistic, enthusiastic, inspiring.
4. Matter-of-fact and methodical. Practical, focused, growth on a strong foundation. Pragmatic.
5. Progressive, flexible, go-with-the-flow. Freedom, active, social, diversity.
6. Idealistic, nurturing, and family-focused. Unselfish and giving to close friends, neighbors, and family. Community recognition and social standing are increased. Family-first is the motto.
7. Intellect, subjective, introspection. Investigates scientific questions and mysteries. Can be a psychic or an awakened Soul.
8. Materialistic, recognition, authority figure, organized. An important businessperson who is efficient and realistic. Professional and balanced.
9. Tolerant, compassionate, humanitarian. Diverse interests include dramas, art, and business. Expanded spiritual or psychological abilities.

The Personal Year, Month, and Day

This is another yearly cycle change. This time, instead of aligning with your birth date, it aligns with the start of a new year. You use your birth date but also the new year number to find this information. October is the earliest you can begin feeling the change in vibration for the Personal Year number. This transition usually completes a few weeks after the start of the New Year.

Your Personal Month is a change that happens every month. When the first of the month begins, your new personal month starts. To find this number you use your birth date and the personal year number calculated above. You can feel the energy change a few days before the end of the previous month and two days after the new month begins the change is complete. This number sets the tone for how the month progresses for you. Your Personal Day cycle changes each day. You use your birth date and your Personal Month number to find this number. The changes occur a few hours before the switch from one day to the next and about two hours after the day starts the change is complete. Your Personal Day Number is like a daily horoscope reading and can reveal the tone of your day.

There are several numerological chart cycles that you can reveal and review to help you learn more about yourself and your future. Sometimes you can find an online calculator that will find out this information for you and provide an interpretation, but many of the calculations are simple and clear. One particular cycle that is great to have an online resource for is your Personal Day number. This way you do not have to do the math each day and interpret your number. The other cycles, however, can be calculated quickly and can help you determine the course of action you will take for that time period.

A few helpful resources for these cycles of change include:
- https://affinitynumerology.com/numerology-tools/power-number-calculator.php
- https://affinitynumerology.com/numerology-tools/numerology-life-period-cycles-tool.php
- https://affinitynumerology.com/numerology-tools/numerology-pinnacles-calculator.php
- https://affinitynumerology.com/numerology-tools/life-challenge-predictions-overlapped-calculator.php
- https://affinitynumerology.com/numerology-tools/life-challenge-predictions-delineated-calculator.php
- https://affinitynumerology.com/numerology-tools/essence-transit-calculator.php
- https://affinitynumerology.com/numerology-tools/personal-year-calculator.php
- https://affinitynumerology.com/numerology-tools/numerology-personal-month-calculator.php
- https://affinitynumerology.com/numerology-tools/personal-day-calendar.php

CHAPTER 10
Numbers For Money, Motivation, And Passion

In addition to having general representations, there are certain qualities that numbers possess. Each number is symbolic and connected to different areas of your life. Sometimes these numbers are related to wealth and money, while other times they are related to how you are motivated, what you are passionate about, etc. The purpose of this chapter is to reveal some of the meaning of different numbers and how they can relate to your life. Also, it is important to remember that sometimes a number represents something that may initially sound "bad," but upon further exploration, it reveals a "good" side to your personality and life. For example, if you cannot hold on to money well, that may be because you are generous and giving to others.

Like other equations for finding your numbers, you will add certain aspects of your information down to a single digit. Sometimes you will reduce down a Master Number, 11 and 22, and sometimes that number will be used in the reading. You have seen this happen throughout this book to this point. In the following sections, you will be guided to either use a Master Number as they appear in their two-digit form, or reduce it further to 2 or 4.

Money

The interpretations below can be applied to any number in your reading, but many people find it best to start with their Life Path Number and find how they will deal with wealth. These numbers and vibrations reveal if you are good at making money, will be gifted money, or how you distribute money. It is revealing how, over the course of your life, you will handle your wealth. It is designed to give you an overview of your financial potential.

Money and Number 1

A number 1 has a financial advantage. You are a leader and money are attracted to you. On the other hand, it is also a number that represents beginnings so you may find yourself starting over again and again. You do not normally get into debt and do not like the feeling of being indebted. Your prosperity rubs off onto the people around you, especially those that you employ.

Money and Number 2

Money is a challenge for you. Wealth is not viewed as traditional money, but wealth to a number 2 is what is shared amongst others. You put others above yourself in many situations, and this includes giving financially to others before giving it to yourself. This can delay your financial stability and lead to disappointment in your life with regards to money. You also enjoy beautiful and luxurious things, which you are willing to go into debt over. Your generosity and materialism can be a major hindrance to your wealth.

Money and Number 3

You are in luck! You make money easy, but you also spend it easily. You may not accumulate money in a bank, but you attract enough of it throughout your life to pay for the things you need and want. Even if you amass a good fortune, you will often feel "a day late and a dollar short" on numerous occasions. Debt is a common occurrence; however, it is easier for a number 3 to get out of debt than other numbers.

Money and Number 4

You are not destined to be poor or indebted, but you will work for every bit of wealth you earn. It is not easy for you to bring in money, but it does come to you. This means you must learn self-discipline and "grit" to stay out of poverty. You probably will never win in the lottery; you are just not lucky with money like that. On the other hand, the money you invest wisely will be likely to grow well.

Money and Number 5

You have a business mind. Stick to a budget and be organized and you will thrive. You are also philanthropic and often treat your employees fairly. You see money as a continual source and it is meant to be spent or given out. Because of this philanthropic nature, the Universe gives you all you need. It is like a karmic expression of gratitude for your kind heart and hard work.

Money and Number 6

You experience abundance in your life. Sometimes this money is given to you, such as an inheritance or gifts from your family. You are the most likely to be gifted money. No matter what you put your mind to, it flourishes. You never have to worry about money coming in. While money is a constant source of abundance, you never experience extreme highs with it. On the other hand, you never face the feeling of extreme lows, either.

Money and Number 7
Your vibe is eccentric, and your finances tend to be as well. Sometimes they are up and other times they are down. You are prone to challenges in this way. It is possible to earn a large sum of money throughout your life, but you do not value money as the best indication of wealth. You value other things in life more than money. It is likely that you have a wild idea that makes you a lot of money. Be careful to watch how you save or spend your money. You have a tendency to hoard or use your money for unethical purposes.

Money and Number 8
You have a wide swing to your financial pendulum. You have the ability to enjoy large sums of money, but you also have the ability to struggle with big losses. It is also important to recognize that in order for you to make money, you need to invest in yourself and your business. You need to spend money to bring it in. Also, you are materialistic and enjoy luxurious things. This has a higher price tag that you must keep up with the keep up this lifestyle.

Money and Number 9
You are not plagued by financial hardships and find making money easy. It takes no effort for you to attract money into your life. On the other hand, you find it challenging to hold on to it for a length of time. You embody the phrase, "penny wise, pound foolish." You are philanthropic and a humanitarian, which tugs at your heart to give what you own away. As a cosmic thank you, everything you touch tends to turn profitable.

If you have a Master Number, reduce it to a single digit to determine your financial vibration. To get a more accurate combination of your financial future, consider applying these interpretations to various numbers in your reading, beyond just your Life Path number. For example, consider applying them to your Pinnacle or Peak years and your Challenges. It can give you an idea of how your wealth will fluctuate over your lifetime and what areas you can focus on to keep yourself in a wealthy and comfortable state of being.

Motivation
You are destined to do great things in life, but in order for you to reach that potential. There are things you need to do to grow. This

requires motivation. Your inner Self wants to become its highest form and live its true potential, but often other parts of your mind and body get in the way of this. This is why it is helpful to find your inner motivation; you can align your actions with what internally motivates you for the best success. Because this is deeper than your surface desires, some people call this a "Soul" number. It dips back into past lives and experiences to find out what is moving your forward. These lessons can be applied to your present state. To find this number, calculate all the vowels in your name. Below is a breakdown of what the numbers are for each letter of the alphabet with each vowel bolded for easier identification:

1	*2*	*3*	*4*	*5*	*6*	*7*	*8*	*9*
A	B	C	D	E	F	G	H	I
J	K	L	M	N	O	P	Q	R
S	T	U	V	W	X	Y	Z	--

Take your full name and reduce it to only the vowels. For example, Jane John Doe becomes Jn Jhn D. Now assign a number to each letter according to the chart above. For example, J = 1, h = 8, n = 5 and D = 4. The equation looks like 1 + 5 + 1 + 8 + 4 + 4 = 23. As with most numerology equations, you are to reduce the double-digit, which is not a Master Number, down to a single digit. For example, 23= 2 + 3 = 5. The Motivation number for Jane John Doe is 5.

Once you determine your Motivation number, learn its vibrational meaning below:

Motivation and Number 1

"I am a pioneer."

You are focused on your goals, are creative, and very independent. Your leadership can be more spiritual in nature because of your understanding of cause and effect or "action and reaction." You have many talents and skills and you like being recognized for them. You seek out opportunity and are a loyal and honest businessperson and friend. You are responsible and necessary for the Universe. On the other hand, you can be less emotionally visible, coming across as cold and uncaring. Be aware of your intentions with your gifts. You may turn into a tyrannical leader or act egotistically. You can be an example to others on how to live an independent and successful life, as long as you stay loyal to your convictions.

Motivation and Number 2
"I am a diplomat."

Diplomacy and cooperation are your motivation. You like being a team player and finding peaceful resolutions. You enjoy helping others find their connection and completeness. Leadership is not a natural role for you, but you are a valued contributor to whatever you do, especially if it appeals to you. Your sensitivity can lead to hurt, especially if you find you are giving too much of yourself because of your generous nature. It is good to give, but do not expect the same generosity in return. That will also lead to hurt. As you develop this skillful balance, you will learn how to be more clairvoyant and see through the masks of others. You are an amazing friend and person and do not need to prove it.

Motivation and Number 3
"I find joy in life."

You love living life! You love to be happy and make others happy. You are social and outgoing. Jokes and humor are something you enjoy and bring with you wherever you go. You are a shining light every place you go, and no one can miss you. You are a strong communicator and thrive in places where you can express yourself; art, writing, singing, presentations, etc. Sometimes you talk too much, not leaving space to listen to others' stories and words. In addition, a love of life can lead to frivolity, so be careful. Do let your joy infect all those around you. Be social and creative.

Motivation and Number 4
"I am aware of others"

Structure, routine, and stability are your motivators. Anything that is in order and in line is great. You love details. You never forget a thing. You are present and aware. You approach life methodically and efficiently. You use your actions to show how something can be done well. Be careful not to come across as a dictator. Sometimes you appear inflexible and rigid. You are destined to accomplish your goals, just be accepting of those around you as individuals. Remember everyone is unique. You are reliable and honest and also great at finances, so becoming an accountant is a great role for you. Innovation and change are hard for you, so try to learn how to relax from time to time. This will help with going with the flow.

Motivation and Number 5

"I am an adventurer and explorer"

Unpredictable, adventurous, and free motivates you. It is not just how you talk about life, but how you live it as well. Change and diversity are important to you, and routine feels like it is holding you down. You can end up jumping from one place or project to the next, so be careful. When you learn to give all your energy to one project, you will enjoy a sense of accomplishment. Travel is a form of therapy for you. Your ideas are wild and bold and sometimes can seem impossible to others. Learn to use your actions to create constructive reactions in line with your goals and desires.

Motivation and Number 6

"I am dedicated to family."

Balance, loyalty, harmony, and responsibility are your motivators. Family and your sense of home are especially important, but this does not mean it is just about your immediate family. Instead, sometimes this sense of home applies to your human connection, for example. It is remarkable how affectionate, understanding, and loving you are. Your past lives have nurtured these traits. Because you have learned such nurturing traits you are nowhere to share those lessons with others. Your diplomacy, gentle nature and a responsible attitude are what you like to be recognized for. Be careful not to shoulder more responsibility that you can handle, especially with your children. Learn how to let them accept their own responsibility. They have to learn how to rise after a fall, which means you do need to let them fall down. Your expression usually is creative, and the acting is a common outlet for you. Just be careful not to fall too far into a fictional existence. Also, you love to show your emotions, but sometimes you let your emotions carry you away. Be careful here. You are willing to sacrifice for causes and people, especially your family. Another warning exists in this great trait; do not sacrifice too much or you will begin to resent those you are trying to help.

Motivation and Number 7

"I am independent"

Analysis, contemplation, and independence are your motivators. Other people are fine surrounding you but you retreat into your mind. Marriage and connection to others are hard. Studying deep subjects and reading a lot are comfortable places for you. You may feel and be different than all the other people around you, and this has to do with your contemplative and meditative state of being. At times people may see you are reserved, stand-off-ish, or timid. You hold your cards tightly against your chest, and no one really knows the true you except yourself. You thrive on finding answers and learning new things, including learning about yourself and your purpose in life. The rhythm of contemporary life is not your "style." Idle chit chat makes you uncomfortable. You are selective in whom you interact with and what you do. You do not like the "mundane." Keep in mind, the wisdom you develop through the course of your reading and studying is meant to be shared. Push yourself to leave your solitary to teach others about all that you know.

Motivation and Number 8

"I am an entrepreneur"

Abundance, power, status, and professional success are your motivators. You are tenacious and determined, able to tackle large projects and events with ease. You love being in charge or large tasks and seeing them through to completion. Prestige and status are important to you. With this often comes wealth and success with material gains. You like to show this success through some of the finer things in life. Watch your attachment to the material side of this life, and make sure your actions are aligned with your values and true Self. Be careful not to judge others too harshly, but do not shun your intuition. Find harmony between the two. The more generous you are to others the more abundance you will receive. Stay true to yourself and life will reward you.

Motivation and Number 9

"I am a philanthropist"

Helping and giving to others and being altruistic are your motivators. You use your wisdom to help others with open arms and heart. You have unconditional love for others and a connection to the spiritual realm. You are naturally optimistic, but others can react negatively to this trait if you are not aware of your environment. Drama runs like a current in Motivation number 9's.

Thankfully, you are also blessed with a streak of courage and boldness that helps you overcome roadblocks in your path. Sometimes you may appear distant, be you have a deep love for people. Sometimes this love for others is so deep you sacrifice your own health in the course of things. Be careful to take care of yourself, saying "no" when necessary for your well-being. You are capable of being the guide, shedding light onto how to include and accept others, as well as how to spread love all around.

Motivation and Number 10
"I have a vision"

Cooperation, illumination, and idealism are your motivators. You love to investigate abstract concepts and study matter. You have an amazing way of comprehending deep concepts and you can heal others with your compassion. You see how this world works and how you can use your knowledge to help. You are a guru, teacher, guide, or master. Your soul is destined to continue the path of the teacher. You are not connected to the material or physical path, but a utopian dream of a connected, equal, and peaceful humanity. Inclusion, understanding, and love for and by all. You are often described as an "old soul." You desire to share all this ancient knowledge you have with everyone you meet. Find ways to let go misunderstandings or confusion about your idealistic visions. Others may not want to listen or comprehend your teachings, but you need to press on anyway. Rely on your inner strength to continue on your path.

Motivation and Number 11
"I am a founder"

accomplishing great tasks and being recognized for your lofty contributions are your motivators. Society comes to you to do great things and you do not disappoint. You are driven to and able to build a valuable and visible contribution to the world. You can become impatient, trying to rush your view of an ideal, equal, and peaceful society. Stay connected to your true self and you will make a large difference in the betterment of humanity. You are also often called an "old soul," like a Motivation number 11. You have acquired a great amount of wisdom through your lives and are sure in your path in life. You are a builder and a founder. When you decide you are going to do something, the Universe provides.

Passion

In addition to what motivates you, there are things you are passionate about, often lying deep inside of you. You may not even know that you are driven or interested in some of these areas. In order to find your Passion number, you need to turn all the letters of your name into numbers, and then identify the number that appears the most often. This is your Passion number. For example, Jane John Doe is 1,1,5,5,1,6,8,5,4,6,5. 5 appears four times, which is the most frequent number in the name. This is Jane John Doe's Passion number. To help you learn about your hidden passions, find your Passion number below.

Passion and Number 1

You need to stand out. You can create anything you decide to bring to life. You are a modern-day superhero, politician, or Olympian.

Passion and Number 2

You are a talented musician with a great appreciation for beautiful things. You are peaceful, organized, sensitive, and intuitive. You are an artist, musician, or work to save our planet.

Passion and Number 3

You are innately able to inspire others. Entertaining and being around great friends and family is enjoyable to you. You are a motivational speaker, artist, writer, or musician, moving people through your expression.

Passion and Number 4

You are able to concentrate and organize better than most people. You love practicality and efficiency as well as the chaos of nature. You are an interior designer, architect, or home organizer.

Passion and Number 5

You love to travel and need to be free. Work and family are important to your happiness. You have trouble sticking to projects, making commitments hard to come by. You are a movie director, translator, in public relations, or a writer.

Passion and Number 6

You must give back to humanity. You are an amazing partner and an idealist. You are a public figure, Reiki master, or teacher.

Passion and Number 7

You are analytical and intuitive. You are great working alone but do enjoy spending time with loved ones. You are able to strike a great balance between solidarity and companionship. You are a philosopher, problem solver, or forever-student.

Passion and Number 8

You are visionary and goal-orientated. You are a leader and strive for success in all that you do. You often enjoy the fruits of your labor. You are a leader in your community, own a business, or a personal trainer.

Passion and Number 9

You are warm, caring, artistic, and independent. Sometimes getting lost in your emotions and dreams, you often find a way to live a good life. You are an artist, innovator, or motivational speaker.

CONCLUSION

Thank you for purchasing *Numerology for the Beginner: Master the Secret Meaning of Numbers and Discover Your Future through Numerology, Astrology, and Tarot Reading*. After learning more about how Numerology works and how you can apply this to your life, now is the time to make a plan for your future. Now is the time to understand your Self and how you can live your best and destined life.

It is hard to learn challenging truths about yourself, and it is even harder to work on balancing your nature. When you are courageous and learn about who you are, even the hidden traits that you have not seen before, you move closer to who you are destined to be. The problem is that it is hard to learn things about yourself that are good and bad. It is hard to try to break habits that you may have been forming for lifetimes. The next step in that process is to continue being courageous. Continue looking into bettering yourself. Determine how you can live your best life now and to come.

The more aligned you live according to your gifts and calling, the more balanced you will be in this life and in the future. Start small and make your improvements one at a time. Each time you work on a part of yourself, the more you grow. Sometimes you will focus on sharing your gifts more or working on a challenging area. No matter what you choose to start with, allow yourself to work and develop towards your purpose. Show yourself compassion and discipline. Achieve your greatness and share it with the world. You are truly a unique vibration, and a force to be reckoned with.

Finally, if you have found this book helpful in any way, a positive review on Amazon is always appreciated!

DESCRIPTION

Have you ever wondered why certain things keep happening to you? Do you keep running into the same types of problems, over and over again, and cannot figure out why or how to stop them? Are you unsure about your purpose in this life? Do you wonder what your future holds for you? It might be time to dig a little deeper into who you are and uncover what makes you, you. There are a few different ways you can learn about yourself, and what your future holds in store, but have you started looking for answers? Are you confused yet?

There are many different methods for uncovering your destiny and your life's path. Numerology is one of those methods. You may have also heard or researched astrology, tarot, and other mystical or spiritual methods for finding yourself. The deeper you dig, the more confusing those methods might become for you. If you are bad at math, especially geometry, you may find astrology nearly impossible to decide on your own. In addition, you need to learn the meanings of several astrological and cosmic entities to be accurate. Tarot is similar in the sense that you need to learn the meaning and interpretation of several different suits and images. It can be confusing and challenging, but numerology is not like that.

Numerology is all about reading your numbers. You have certain, recurring numbers throughout your life that influence your past, present, and future. And thankfully, these numbers are not complex. In fact, they are pretty much only numbers one through nine. This means, once you learn these nine vibrations, you can read any part of your life well. There are six main numbers related to your birthdate and your name. These six reveal various truths and hidden secrets about you. But beyond that, there are many other revelations in your numbers. You can learn things like how you handle or interact with money, what motivates you, and even your passion that lurks underneath.

It can be scary to dig into your deeper self and uncover why you are or are not bringing to life things you need and desire. It can be hard to hear that you are not good with money or relationships. It can be hard to discover why you struggle in social situations or wonder about your purpose in life. But when you open yourself up to the answers, there is infinite opportunity to live the life you were born to enjoy.

From the start of this book, begin to uncover all mystical secrets, such as;
- The history behind numerology
- The basic of the science
- How the numbers relate to the various aspects of your Self
- What patterns of numbers reveal
- How your numbers relate to your phases in life and when those phases occur
- The connection of numerology to astrology and tarot
- How your numbers reveal your relationships
- The numbers related to your interactions with wealth, motivation, your passions.
- And much, much more!